THE
ALASKA FLYING
EXPEDITION

THE U.S. ARMY'S 1920 NEW YORK TO NOME FLIGHT

Airplane Flight From
New York to Nome Is
Postponed Ten Days

Sergeant W. W. McLaughlin has been advised that the aerial flight from New York to Nome has been postponed by the War Department from July 5 to July 15. This will mean that the airplanes will arrive in Wrangell on July 18th or 19th.

The old and the new modes of transportation in the Yukon. Two of the Black Wolf Squadron aircraft at Dawson City with a dog sled in the foreground. DAWSON CITY MUSEUM AND HISTORICAL SOCIETY, LOUISE BLACK COLL. PH984R-76-13

THE ALASKA FLYING EXPEDITION

THE U.S. ARMY'S 1920 NEW YORK TO NOME FLIGHT

BY STAN COHEN

Plane No. 1 piloted by Capt. St. Clair Streett at Mitchel Field before takeoff. CAM

Pictorial Histories Publishing Co., Inc.
Missoula, Montana

LIBRARY OF CONGRESS
CATALOG CARD NO. 98-65348

ISBN 1-57510-041-X

First Printing: April 1998

Layout: Leslie Maricelli
Cover Graphics: Mike Egeler, Egeler Design
Cover Artwork: Jim Farmer

Back Cover:

Top Map: Courtesy Alaska Aviation Heritage Museum, Anchorage
Middle Items: Courtesy Alaska State Museum, Juneau
Bottom DH-4 Profile: Courtesy Mike Egeler, Egeler Design

Pictorial Histories Publishing Co., Inc.
713 South Third West, Missoula, Montana 59801

 # Introduction

It had been 17 years since the Wright Brothers flew their aeroplane at Kitty Hawk. There had been many aviation firsts in the ensuing years, and more were to come in the 1920s and 1930s. America seemed to be at the forefront of this great revolution in transportation.

One of the most daring aviation adventures took place in the summer of 1920 when eight daredevil U.S. Army Air Service fliers made a historic flight from Long Island, New York, to the barren coast on the Bering Sea and the famous Alaskan gold mining camp of Nome. The approximate round-trip distance was 9,000 miles, much of it over uncharted country.

The flight, involving four modified World War I vintage DH-4B bombers, was inspired by Brig. Gen. Billy Mitchell, then assistant chief of the Army Air Service, who had spent some time in the wild Alaskan territory in the early 1900s. Mitchell was a strong advocate for promoting Alaska as America's first line of defense. The flight, if successful, would help to establish an effective aerial route to Alaska and on to Asia. It would chart and photograph inaccessible areas of Alaska, demonstrate the reliability of the airplane for long-distance transportation and the hauling of troops by air, and establish aviation cooperation between the United States and Canada.

The trip northward was completed only after overcoming many unforeseen obstacles. It was not the day of emergency landing fields or even prepared main landing fields. The pilots had to endure incredible types of weather in their open cockpits, including the airmen's greatest menace: fog. There were no modern compasses, and more than 2,000 miles of the flight lay over virgin territory far removed from human habitation, over the dreary, impenetrable swamps of the Yukon, over jagged mountain peaks and snow covered glaciers.

Capt. St. Clair Streett, the mission's leader, was asked by newspaper reporters what the purpose of the flight was. He answered, "Yesterday a month was required to reach the Yukon. If our expedition succeeds, it will prove that the Yukon is but three days distant—by airplane."

In all it took three months to make the round trip, with 112 actual flying hours. And all this without a serious mishap. This would be the first penetration by air into portions of the Canadian provinces of Alberta and British Columbia, the Yukon Territory and Alaska.

It is a story that has had too brief a mention in several modern publications. Streett's story in the May 1922 issue of *National Geographic* magazine, *The First Alaskan Air Expedition* is the best-written description of the event.

This book will tell the story in a log of each leg of the trip accompanied by surviving photographs of the journey.

Stan Cohen
April 1998

Airplane Insignias

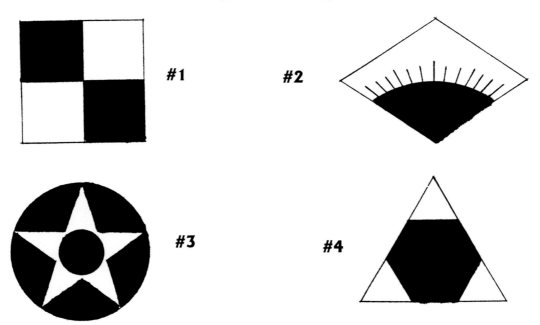

 *Acknowledgments*

Sources in both the United States and Canada were contacted for photos and information. However, this book could not have been finished without the great help of Trelle A. Morrow of Prince George, British Columbia, who provided photos of the British Columbia segment of the flight and wrote the articles on Prince George and Hazelton. He also provided copies of the 1920 Air Service Newsletters of which I was not aware.

I wish to thank the following for their help: Margaret Weatherly of the Reeve Aleutian Airways office in Anchorage; India Sparty, librarian at the Alaska State Library in Juneau; Steve Henrickson, curator of collections, Alaska State Museum, Juneau; Diane Brenner, archivist at the Anchorage Museum of History and Art; Dave Menard at the U.S. Air Force Museum, Dayton, Ohio; Al Lloyd, of the Boeing Aircraft Company, Seattle, Washington; Theresa Thibault, Wrangell Museum; Steve Hubbard, Fargo Public Library; Annita Andricks, Erie County Historical Society; Rebecca Looney, Cradle of Aviation Museum, Garden City, New York; Heather Jones, Yukon Archives, Whitehorse; Nadine Small, chief archivist, Saskatchewan Archives Board, Saskatoon; Mavie Dorsch, Winona County Historical Society; Dr. Sandra Thomson, director, and Lori Enns of the Provincial Archives of Alberta; Laura Kosell of the Carrie M. McLain Memorial Museum, Nome; Ted Spencer of the Alaska Aviation Heritage Museum, Anchorage; and the staffs of the Grand Rapids Public Library and the Archives, Raymond M. Blasco M.D. Memorial Library, Erie, Pa., and the Erie County Historical Society; Alaska and Polar Regions Department, University of Alaska Fairbanks. Leslie Maricelli did the layout and design, Mike Egeler produced the graphics using Jim Farmer's original front cover painting and Dennis Swibold of the University of Montana Journalism School did the editing.

About the Photographs

The bulk of the photographs in this book were obtained from the Reeve Aleutian Airways collection in Anchorage. They were taken by Lt. Clifford M. Nutt and are credited RAA. The rest of the photographs noted as follows:

AC—Author's Collection

AHL—Alaska Historical Library, Juneau

YA—Yukon Archives, Whitehorse

AFM—U.S. Air Force Museum, Dayton, Ohio

BA—Boeing Archives, Seattle, Washington

AMHA—Anchorage Museum of History & Art, Anchorage

CAM—Cradle of Aviation Museum, Garden City, N.Y.

SI—Smithsonian Institution, Washington, D.C.

PAA—Provincial Archives of Alberta, Edmonton

TMC—Trelle Morrow Collection, Prince George, B.C.

UAA—Alaska and Polar Region Archives, Rasmuson Library, University of Alaska, Fairbanks

Other photographs are acknowledged by the source.

Contents

Introduction .... *v*

Acknowledgments .... *vi*

The Flight *1*

Mitchel Field *4*

The Participants *7*

DH-4 .... *15*

The Takeoff to Erie *19*

To Grand Rapids *27*

To Winona and Minneapolis *31*

To Fargo *35*

To Portal *39*

To Saskatoon *41*

To Edmonton *45*

To Jasper *49*

To Prince George and Hazelton *53*

To Wrangell *61*

To Whitehorse *67*

To Dawson *73*

To Fairbanks *75*

To Ruby and Nome *85*

The Trip Home *95*

DFC for Captain Streett *106*

"Close Up" Pen Pictures of the Alaskan Flight *108*

Bibliography *112*

About the Authors and Artist *112*

*"At Nome, Captain Streett and his men stood on the
threshold of Asia and could have crossed in an hour
and a half. A fully equipped air force based in Alaska,
was essential to the defense of America."*

General Billy Mitchell

Trip Log 1920

North

From	To	Arrived	Distance in Miles	Cumulative Miles
Mitchell Field	Erie, PA	July 17	352	--
Erie, PA	Grand Rapids, MI	July 21	300	652
Grand Rapids, MI	Winona, MN	July 22	310	962
Winona, MN	Minneapolia, MN	July 22	100	1062
Minneapolis, MN	Fargo, ND	July 24	225	1287
Fargo, ND	Portal, ND	July 25	290	1577
Portal, ND	Saskatoon, Sask.	July 26	280	1857
Saskatoon, Sask.	Edmonton, Alb.	July 27	300	2157
Edmonton, Alb.	Return –FOG	July 31	120	2277
Edmonton, Alb.	Jasper, Alb.	August 1	200	2477
Jasper, Alb.	Prince George, BC	August 2	215	2692
Prince George, BC	Hazelton, BC	August 13	220	2912
Hazelton, BC	Wrangell, AK	August 14	210	2133
Wrangell, AK	Whitehorse, YT	August 16	315	3457
Whitehorse, YT	Dawson, YT	August 18	250	3707
Dawson, YT	Fairbanks, AK	August 19	275	3982
Fairbanks, AK	Ruby, AK	August 20	240	4222
Ruby, AK	Nome, AK	August 23	305	4527

South

From	To	Arrived	Distance in Miles	Cumulative Miles
Nome	Ruby	August 31	305	4832
Ruby	Fairbanks	August 31	240	5072
Fairbanks	Dawson	September 1	275	5347
Dawson	Whitehorse	September 5	250	5597
Whitehorse	Ret., snow, fog	September 9	275	5872
Whitehorse	Telegraph Creek	September 10	235	6107
Telegraph Creek	Ret., snow, fog	September 19	220	6327
Telegraph Creek	Hazelton, BC	September 29	230	6557
Hazelton, BC	Prince George, BC	October 4	220	6777
Prince George, BC	Jasper	October 8	215	6992
Jasper	Edmonton	October 8	200	7192
Edmonton	Saskatoon	October 10	300	7492
Saskatoon	Portal	October 11	280	7772
Portal	Fargo	October 11	290	8062
Fargo	Winona	October 14	325	8387
Winona	Grand Rapids	October 16	310	8697
Grand Rapids	Erie	October 18	300	8997
Erie	Mitchel Field	October 20	352	9349

The Flight

The flight to Nome came at a time of extreme controversy among American military leaders as to the future of military aviation.

World War I proved the value of aviation in both an offensive and defensive capability. But by 1920, with America thinking only of peace, the entire military establishment was scaled down.

Gen. Billy Mitchell had come back from France in early 1919 as a great war hero and undoubtedly the most knowledgeable aviation expert in America's armed forces. He was waging an uphill battle to place military aviation in its rightful place: on an equal footing with both the Army and Navy.

Col. H.H. "Hap" Arnold reflected in 1919: "General Mitchell came back to a nation which was tired of war, not a fertile soil for his teachings and pleadings for air power. Mitchell took office on March 1, 1919, as assistant to the new chief of the Air Service of the U.S. Army, Gen. Charles T. Menoker.

In the late spring of 1919, a mission headed by Benedict Crowell, assistant secretary of war and director of munitions during the war, was sent to Europe to study aviation. It was to formulate a policy for the administration. The seven members of the mission, in their aim to place American aviation in the front rank among nations, unanimously recommended:

"The concentration of the air activities of the United States, civilian, naval and military, within the direction of a single Government agency created for the purpose, coequal in importance and in representation with The Departments of War, Navy and Commerce."

But there was little support for the idea. Even General Pershing spoke out against the establishment of a separate air service, much to the disappointment of General Mitchell. However, Gen. Benjamin Foulois, who was chief of the air service in France during the war, spoke out in favor of a separate air service. He stated his position before a congressional committee on Dec. 5, 1919:

"I believe at this time we should organize it as a department, but not with a Cabinet officer. I believe it should be a separate department, however. On the other hand, I think its importance is such that it will be a Cabinet position eventually. I think its importance is co-equal with that of the army in the national defense scheme at present, and will soon be superior to that of the navy."

In the meantime, Mitchell was pioneering government regulations of aerial traffic and promoting commercial aviation. He wrote in the *U.S. Air Service* in the spring of 1919:

"The Atlantic is going to be crossed and within a short time we shall have regular airplane mail transportation between American and Europe. ...We no longer measure distance by miles but by time. The commercial traveler henceforth will read the new air time table and find not distance by miles, but that Chicago is four hours from New York, or that Los Angeles is twenty-eight hours from Boston."

To promote his ideas, Mitchell inaugurated the first transcontinental air reliability contest. Thirty Army planes started from San Francisco and an equal number from New York. It was also an effort to promote a coast-to-coast airmail service.

He wrote to his friend, "Hap" Arnold: "I am very anxious to push through a flight to Alaska with land planes." He advised: "Better get oriented along the line as to the possibilities from your department north. This might develop into a round-the-world flight."

"Having demonstrated that we could go across the United States," wrote Mitchell in 1919, "we wanted to demonstrate that we could establish an airway to Alaska and Asia."

Thus was born the idea for the first U.S. Army flight to Alaska.

Brig. Gen. Billy Mitchell and his group of planners in the Air Service set about planning for the trip late in 1919. By the spring of 1920 they had selected a route. General Menoker and Secretary of War Newton B. Baker approved the flight the Air Service billed as "The Year's Greatest Aerial Event."

The expedition consisted of four World War I era DH-4 airplanes. In Plane No. 1 would be flight commander Capt. St. Clair Streett, and Sgt. Edmund Henriques, a mechanic. In Plane No. 2 was 1st Lt. Clifford C. Nutt, pilot and second in command, and 1st

Lt. Erik H. Nelson, navigating and engineering officer. In Plane No. 3 was 2nd Lt. Clarence E. Crumrine, pilot and photographic officer, and mechanic Sgt. James D. Long. Apparently, Long was picked at the last moment to replace a mechanic named Sgt. Albert T. Vierra, who is pictured in several of the pre-flight photos. In Plane No. 4 was 2nd Lt. Ross C. Kirkpatrick, the pilot and information officer, and Master Sgt. Joseph E. English, a mechanic.

The destination would be Nome, Alaska, more than 4,000 miles from the expedition takeoff at Mitchel Field on New York's Long Island. The date set was July 5, 1920, but due to complications the flight did not take off until July 15.

Three months before the expedition set out from Mitchel Field, Capt. Howard T. Douglas went over the proposed route and prepared landing fields, some of which were cut in virgin forests. Others were laid out in small stump-littered clearings and on river beds. He also arranged for supplies along their route. His liaison in the Canadian portion was Captain H.A. LeRoyer of the Canadian Air Force.

The official name of the group was The Alaska Flying Expedition, but it also went by the Black Wolf Squadron for the emblem painted on the side of each aircraft. It has also been called The New York to Nome Flight.

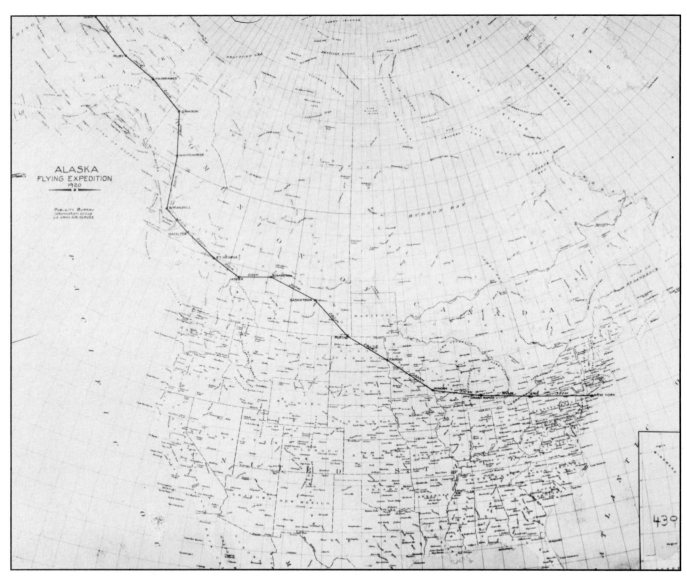

The flight from Mitchel Field to Nome, Alaska.

Brig. Gen. William "Billy" Mitchell

No one had a greater interest in the successful completion of the Alaska Flying Expedition than Brig. Gen. William "Billy" Mitchell. At the time he was assistant chief of the U.S. Army Air Service and the originator of the idea to fly to Nome and return.

The father of the modern Air Force was born in 1879 in Nice, France, of American parents. He was from a prominent family of Milwaukee, Wisconsin. He enlisted in the Army as a private during the Spanish-American War and rose rapidly in the Signal Corps branch, which first controlled the development of aviation in the U.S. Army.

In 1902, he was sent to Alaska to construct a telegraph line through hundreds of miles of trackless wilderness. The experience formulated his idea that Alaska held a prominent place in the defense of the North American continent.

Mitchell learned to fly in 1916 and became air adviser to Gen. John Pershing in World War I. Mitchell commanded several large air units in combat, including the largest concentration of Allied air power during the Battle of the Argonne. He became a brigadier general by the end of the war.

After the war, Mitchell became the leading advocate of an independent air force. He found natural resistance among leaders of the Army and Navy, and appealed to the public through books, magazine articles, newspaper interviews and speeches. Because airplanes were then limited in size and range, many people thought his claims for air power were exaggerated. But he persuaded many others, especially after a 1921 experiment in which he sunk several ships by air attack. He repeated this success twice in later attacks.

But Mitchell failed to achieve his goal, perhaps partly because he was frequently violent in his arguments and bitter in his condemnation of superiors who did not agree with him. He was court-martialed in 1925 for defiance of his superiors and resigned from the Army rather than accept a five-year suspension.

Early in World War II, events confirmed many of Mitchell's predictions. In 1946, Congress authorized the Medal of Honor for Mitchell, who had died 10 years before.

Mitchell in France during WWI. A German airplane in the background. AC

Brig. Gen. William "Billy" Mitchell. AC

 *Mitchel Field*

The Alaska Flying Expedition took off from the historic Mitchel Field in Nassau County, Long Island, New York. During the Revolutionary War this area served as an army enlistment center known as Hempstead Plains. During both the War of 1812 and the Mexican War it was an infantry training post. In the Civil War it was known as Camp Winfield Scott. It was called Camp Black during the Spanish-American War.

Camp Mills was located on the site during World War I. The 42nd (Rainbow) Division, including the famous Fighting 69th Regiment, trained here. On July 16, 1918, the camp was renamed Mitchel Field for Maj. John Purroy Mitchel, former mayor of New York City, who had been killed in an aircraft accident on July 6.

In addition to the New York to Nome flight, other aviation "firsts" took place at Mitchel Field. In 1923,

two airplane world speed records were established there, and the first parachute contest was held. The first transcontinental airmail flight took off from the field in 1924. In 1929, famed aviator Jimmy Doolittle gave the first public demonstration of "blind flying."

Mitchel Field was a center of air tactical training, troop garrisoning, supply and medical treatment during World War II. The base was deactivated in 1961.

In 1999, part of the former military complex will open as the Museums at Mitchel Center, featuring an outstanding collection of military aircraft and spacecraft to be known as the Cradle of Aviation Museum. The Leroy R. and Rose W. Grumman Imax Dome Theater to be built there will be among the largest and most advanced motion picture theaters in the world.

Mitchel Field in 1920. CAM

Mitchel Field 1933. CAM

The crews at Mitchel Field dressed up for inspection. From left: Streett, Nutt, Kirkpatrick, Nelson, Crumrine, English, Henriques and Vierra (who was replaced by Long). RAA

The Participants

The leader of the Black Wolf Squadron, Capt. St. Clair Streett, had a long and illustrious career with the U.S. Army Air Service, U.S. Army Air Corps, U.S. Army Air Forces and the U.S. Air Force.

Streett was born in Washington, D.C., on Oct. 6, 1893. After graduating from high school, he enlisted in December 1916 as a sergeant in the Signal Corps and was assigned to the Curtiss School in Newport News, Virginia, as a flying cadet. In September 1917, after training in Ohio, he was commissioned a first lieutenant in the Aviation Section of the Signal Officers' Reserve Corps.

In December 1917, he was sent to France and assigned to the Fifth Pursuit Group at St. Remy. Streett served with the American occupation forces in Germany before returning to the United States in August 1919. He was promoted to captain in the Signal Officers' Reserve Corps in November 1918 and received a Regular Army commission as a first lieutenant in the Air Service on July 1, 1920.

His leadership of the New York-to-Nome flight resulted in his being awarded the Distinguished Flying Cross in 1926. After his return to New York in 1920, he was appointed assistant to Brig. Gen. Billy Mitchell, the assistant chief of the Air Service. In July 1922, he became commanding officer of the headquarters detachment at Bolling Field, Washington, D.C.

In January 1924, he was named assistant chief of the Airways Section in the Office of the Chief of the Air Corps. In September 1925, he entered the Air Corps Tactical School at Langley Field, Virginia, graduating the following June. Afterward he was transferred to Selfridge Field, Michigan, and appointed commanding officer of the First Pursuit Group headquarters. In March 1928, he was assigned to Wright Field, Ohio, as a test pilot and chief of the Flying Branch.

During the next three years he spent time at service schools, including the Army War College, from which he graduated in 1935. In the late 1930s and early '40s, he was posted to the War Plans Division. He also attended the Naval War College and became commanding officer, as a lieutenant colonel, of the 11th Bombardment Group at Hickam Field, Hawaii.

During World War II, he was deputy chief of the Army Air Forces; commander of the Third Air Force, the Second Air Force, the 13th Air Force; and deputy commander of the Continental Air Forces (later the Strategic Air Command), of which he was also deputy commander until 1947.

In January 1947, he was made chief of the Military Personnel Procurement Office, and in 1948 was appointed the Air Inspector and later the Deputy Inspector General. His final assignments before retiring in 1952 were as deputy commander of the Air Material Command and special assistant to the commanding general of the Air Material Command.

Streett was promoted to brigadier general in 1946 and major general in 1948. He was awarded the Distinguished Service Medal with two Oak Leaf Clusters, the Legion of Merit, the Distinguished Flying Cross, the Air Medal and the Purple Heart.

General Streett died on Sept. 29, 1970, leaving his wife, Mary, and a son, Lt. Col. St. Clair Streett Jr.

Streett during WWI. AFM

Erik Nelson had adventures long before he took off from Mitchel Field in 1920. He would be a pioneer in both military and civilian aviation. He was co-pilot on Plane No. 2 and navigating and engineering officer for the entire flight.

Nelson was born in Sweden in 1888 and educated at the Stockholm Technical Institute. He shipped as a seaman, sailing twice around the world. For five years, he sailed under almost every flag in the world. He came to the United States in 1909 and became a citizen in 1914.

He returned to engineering as an automotive mechanic, making one of the first transcontinental auto trips from New York to San Francisco. He then became affiliated with aviation as a mechanic, flying with barnstormers. In World War I, he enlisted as a private and, on learning to fly, was commissioned. He became a flying instructor and soon was rated the best DH-4 flyer in the Air Service.

Early in 1919, he made a 4,000-mile round trip flight from the Gulf of Mexico to the Pacific Coast, during which he participated in making the first aerial photographs ever taken of the Grand Canyon. That summer, he led a squadron of planes on a 7,000-mile recruiting tour for the Air Service, visiting 32 cities.

Nelson served at McCook Field from 1921 to 1923, and in 1922 he won the two-engine bomber race at Selfridge Field. In 1923, he led a 6,000-mile over-ocean survey flight from Texas to Puerto Rico to Washington, D.C., and then back.

In 1924, Nelson participated in the historic Douglas Round-The-World Flight. In preparation for the flight, Nelson was assigned as special consultant to Donald Douglas to help design and build the Douglas World Cruiser used on the flight.

Nelson resigned his commission in 1928 and became a sales manager and later a vice-president and director of The Boeing Company. He was largely responsible for forming the Boeing Air Transport Co., later to become United Air Lines. He also helped develop the Model 247, 40B-4, P-12, F4B, 80-A, and the B-29.

After retiring from Boeing in 1936, he worked as an aviation consultant. During World War II, he worked in aircraft development, especially on the B-29 bomber. He was appointed a brigadier general in October 1945.

After his second retirement in 1946, he was named technical adviser to Swedish Intercontinental Airlines.

General Nelson died at his home in Hawaii in 1981. His awards and decorations include the Distinguished Service Medal, Distinguished Flying Cross, the Legion of Merit with Bronze Oak Leaf Cluster, World War I Medal, European Campaign Ribbon, Asiatic Campaign Ribbon with five stars, Macay Trophy, the Legion of Honor of France, the Order of the Sword of Sweden and other decorations.

Nelson during World War I. BA

At Mitchel Field. From left: Crumrine, Vierra, English, Henriques, Streett, Kirkpatrick, Nutt and Nelson. CAM

Just before takeoff at Mitchel Field. CAM

Top left: Lieutenant Crumrine
of Plane No. 3. RAA

Top right: Lieutenant Crumrine
and Sergeant Vierra. RAA

Bottom: Sergeant English and
Lieutenant Kirkpatrick of Plane
No. 4. RAA

Clifford Cameron Nutt, left and Eric Nelson, right. RAA

Captain Streett and Captain Albert Wright, who was General Mitchell's aide. RAA

From left: Sergeants Henriques, English and Vierra. RAA

Sergeant English and Lieutenant Kirkpatrick. RAA

Plane No. 3 with Lieutenant Crumrine and Sergeant Vierra. RAA

Captain Streett.

Lieutenant Nutt.

Lieutenant Crumrine.

Lieutenant Kirkpatrick.

Lieutenant Crumrine.

Lieutenant Kirkpatrick.

Captain Douglas and a travelling companion.

Captain H.A. LeRoyer of the Canadian Air Force, who was Captain Douglas' liaison for the Canadian portion of the flight.

Nutt's Plane No. 2, the *Kittie IV.*

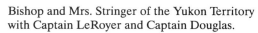

Bishop and Mrs. Stringer of the Yukon Territory with Captain LeRoyer and Captain Douglas.

DH-4

The aircraft chosen to fly the dangerous 10,000-mile round trip was the reliable DeHavilland DH-4. Although it was originally a British combat aircraft design, it was redesigned in the United States in 1917 for the Liberty engine. The plane was used by the United States Army Air Service in France primarily for observation, day bombing and artillery spotting.

It earned the name "The Flaming Coffin" because of the supposed ease with which it could be shot down in flames. In reality, only eight of the 33 DH-4s lost in combat by the Air Service burned as they fell. This was no greater a percentage than for the French- and British-built airplanes used by the AEF in France.

The DH-4 was the only U.S.-built airplane to get into combat during World War I. By the end of the war, 3,431 had been delivered to the Air Service, most of which were built by the Dayton-Wright Airplane Co. Of these, 1,213 had been shipped to France and 417 had gotten into combat. A total of 4,846 were built in the United States by the end of the production run in March 1919.

The plane was a reliable machine with good speed and load capability. It had high aspect ratio wings and a large tail perched at the end of a long fuselage. It was stable in flight and relatively pleasant to fly. It could also take a lot of punishment, as will be seen in the following chapters.

However, there were drawbacks to the wartime model, so the Air Service had a program that would make the plane safer and stronger. Between 1919 and 1923, more than 1,500 surplus planes were modified by moving the gas tank immediately behind the engine, thus lessening the danger to the pilot, whose position in the earlier model was between the motor and the tank.

Thus was born the DH-4B model, the one used on the Alaska Flying Expedition.

The DH-4 in its many models and conversions was the dominant post-war aircraft for many years for both military and civilian use because of the numbers left over at the end of the war.

The DH-4Bs were powered by the famous Liberty "12" V type, 420 h.p. engine. It was developed in the United States by two engineers holed up in the Willard Hotel in Washington, D.C. From its initial production start in 1917 to its production end in March 1919, 20,478 were built by the American automobile industry. They were in use until replaced by more modern engines in July 1929. Their use was not confined to aircraft. Boats, tanks and even wind machines on Hollywood sets used the engine in some modified form.

The Liberty combined large cubic displacement with a relatively low compression ratio and low RPM to achieve its designed horsepower.

The engine proved reliable on the four DH-4Bs used on the Alaska Flying Expedition. Most of the problems that plagued the flight were due to takeoffs or landings from unsuitable air strips. The engines were of minimal concern but did require a lot of maintenance due to stressful flying conditions in bad weather.

Each plane could carry 117 gallons of gas and 12 gallons of oil, which gave them a cruising range of four to five hours, depending on weather. Each plane had a black wolf's head painted on its side and displayed a different symbol to distinguish it from the others. In addition to small repair parts, the planes also carried tools and personal gear. Coming back, the planes were loaded down with gifts collected along the way, including dogs.

SPECIFICATIONS

Weight Empty	2,591 lbs.
Gross Weight	3,782 lbs.
Span	42' 7"
Length	29' 11"
Height	9' 8"
Ceiling	15,800'
Speed, Max.	128 mph
Speed, Cruise	90 mph
Range	400 miles
Cost	$11,250

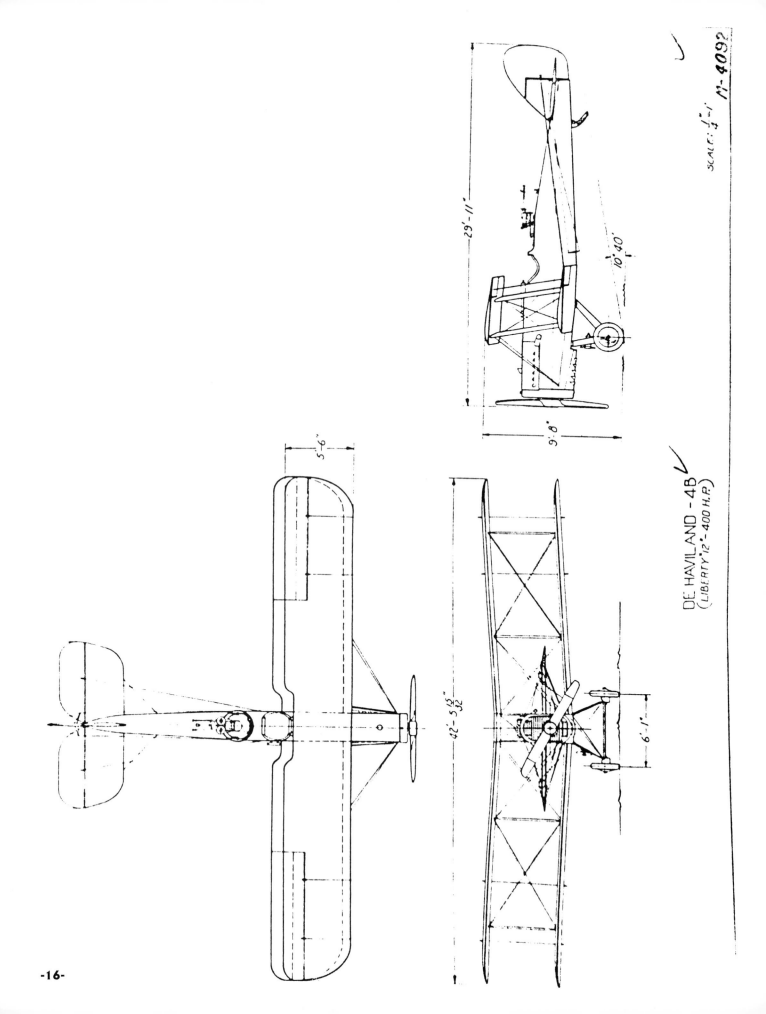

N-4092

SCALE: $\frac{1}{4}"=1'$

29'-11"

10'-40'

9'-8"

5'-6"

42'-5 $\frac{5}{32}$"

6'-1"

DE HAVILAND - 4B
(LIBERTY 12"-400 H.P.)

The four planes lined up at Mitchel Field before takeoff. From left: No. 2, 3, 1 and 4. AC

Putting the finishing touches on Kirkpatrick's plane before takeoff. CAM

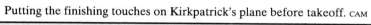

The Hellgate Bridge that connects Randalls Island Park with Queens over the East River, as seen from Nutt's vantage point. RAA

Photos taken by Lt. Nutt as he passed over New York City.

A good view of lower Manhattan. RAA

Dignitaries at the takeoff on July 15, 1920: General Peyton March (top left), General John J. Pershing (top right) and Generals Mitchell and Pershing by the flag at the bottom. RAA

Army Planes Wait Here For Capt. St. Clair Street, Forced To Land Near Scranton—Arrives Late Today

CAPT. ST. CLAIR STREET, U.S.A.

Photograph of Capt. St. Clair Street in machine which he is piloting from Elmhurst, near Scranton, to Erie today. Capt. Street, who is in command of the four army planes on a flight from New York to Nome, Alaska, became lost in a heavy fog just west of New York city yesterday afternoon and headed south, finally landing at Elmhurst. He immediately wired Lieut. C. C. Nutt, second in command, to hold other planes here over night and wait for his arrival some time today before continuing to Grand Rapids, Mich., the next scheduled stop. Three of the army planes are waiting to get away at Exposition Park today, having reached here at 5:20, Eastern Standard time, (official) yesterday evening.

Erie Daily Times
July 16

ALASKAN FLIERS TO STAY IN CITY TODAY

Tno of Planes Awaits Arrival of Captain Street Before Continuing Westward Journey

HE IS STILL HELD BY ACCIDENT

BULLETIN

Scranton, Pa., July 16. Captain St. Clair Streett, commanding officer of the transcontinental flying expedition, whose plane was slightly damaged when a fog compelled him to descend at Elmhurst, near here, will be able to resume his journey to Erie this morning.

Failing to get away yesterday because the parts necessary to repair his damaged plane had not arrived, Captain St Clair Streett commanding the flying expedition from New York to Alaska, will resume his flight today for this city, where three planes completing the squadron safely landed Thursday afternoon. The planes will probably start on the second lap of their trip tomorrow morning.

Captain Streett was forced to descend at Elmhurst at sundown Thursday after the three other fliers were lost in a fog which enveloped them from the time they made the jump at Mitchel field. The axle on his plane was broken in landing and he wired to Mitchel field for necessary parts.

The fliers yesterday spent most of the afternoon in cleaning their machines and making ready for the second lap of their 9,000 mile journey. No further messages were received from Captain Streett concerning his plans and the fliers doubted whether he would make his appearance on the field at the Exposition grounds before noon. Shipments of freight were being delayed, they said, and it would require considerable time to repair the damaged part of Streett's plane. The three here will not resume the trip until the arrival of Captain Streett.

Sunshine and no threat of rain brought a large crowd to the Exposition grounds in the hope of witnessing the start of the flight to Grand Rapids, Michigan, the second top. Disappointed when Lieutenant Kirkpatrick announced no flight would be made, the crowds collected around the three planes and bombarded the fliers with questions. The trio, in good humor, answered them with a smiling readiness that earned them the distinction of being "the nicest flying men who ever landed in Erie."

Erie Daily Times, July 16

Street Makes Erie; Aviators Off for Alaska

Commander Landed at Exposition Grounds at 12:55 P. M., Erie Time.

Capt. St Clair Street, commanding the New York to Alaska War Department aviation flight, who became lost in a fog Thursday and finally landed at Elmhurst, near Scranton, while the other three 'planes of his command came on to Erie arriving safely Thursday evening, landed at Exposition Park at 12:55 p. m., Erie time, today.

Arrangements had been made for a supply of oil and gasoline and the work of preparing the fourth machine for the next "hop off" to Grand Rapids, Mich., was started without delay.

It is expected that the four 'planes, with Capt. Street again in active command, will get away during the afternoon. They had not started up to the time this edition went to press.

Oil and gasoline was put aboard the crafts yesterday and mechanicians made sure that everything was in tip-top shape.

Hundreds of persons made trips yesterday to the Exposition grounds to view the machines which are attempting to establish a mail route to Alaska, in an effort to cut down mail deliveries.

The three machines came through in a little more than five hours, establishing a record of more than 72 miles an hour for the trip.

Wilkes-Barre, Pa., July 17.— Capt. St. Clair Street, commander of the Alaskan flying expedition, who was lost in the fog in the first lap of the journey, forced to a landing at Elmhurst, near Scranton, in which an axle was broken, resumed his flight today, taking the air at 4:10 a. m. (Eastern time), heading for Erie, Pa.

Erie Daily Times July 17

Field at Erie, Pennsylvania. RAA

Repairing Streett's plane after he joined the group at Erie.
RAA

Nutt's plane getting the final touches before takeoff at Erie.
RAA

THREE PLANES BOUND FOR ALASKA LAND HERE; BEAT TELEGRAM TO CITY

Fourth in Group Blazing Aerial Mail Trail Is Forced to Land Near Scranton

TRIP FROM MITCHEL FIELD IS MADE IN FIVE HOURS

Erie Canteen Workers Greet Men on Landing; Will Remain Here Today

Three of four giant de Haviland planes blazing a mail trail from New York to Alaska, landed here safely late yesterday afternoon at the Exposition grounds on the first lap of the 9,000 mile journey. The fourth plane, piloted by Captain St Clair Streett, in command of the expedition, was forced to descend at Elmhurst, Pa., near Scranton, at sundown. Captain Streett became separated from his companions about 15 miles from the starting point at Mitchel field, L. I., shortly after noon yesterday.

The trip from Mitchel filed covered a distance of 352 miles and was made in 5 hours and 5 minutes, the aviators landing here at 5:35 p. m., showing an average speed of 72 miles an hour. Lieutenant C. E. Crumrine piloted plane No. 3, the first to appear on the horizon and to take the ground. Sergeant J. D. Long manned the plane as mechanic. Lieutenant Ross Kirkpatrick and Sergeant Joseph English manned plane No. 4, the second to land, and Lieutenant C. C. Nutt, second in command, and Lieutenant E. H. Nelson were pilots for the "Katie 4," as their plane is christened. The "Katie 4" circled the Exposition grounds before landing.

Hampered by a stiff heavy fog which covered the ground for a hundred miles from their "jump," and encountering stiff northwesterly winds, the aviators were thrown from their course several times and failed to achieve the 100 mile an hour average which was part of their schedule. Lieutenant Nutt at one point along the flight had almost directed a landing when he determined to attempt the completion of the first lap without a stop.

A large crowd whose eyes were riveted on the eastern horizon for hours before the planes put in appearance dwindled to a handful of faithful Red Cross canteen workers patiently holding the thermosed coffee, sandwiches and cigarettes, when a flock of ominous black clouds gathered under the sun. Their threatening aspect seemed an assurance that the expedition had again postponed its flight and even the American Legion squad motored its way home for the third time within the month, but quickly put in an appearance when the announcement of the planes' arrival was telephoned about the city.

Lieutenant Kirkpatrick of Plane 2, alighting from his cubby hole, shouted for The Dispatch representative and handed him a sealed container enclosing a copy of the New York Times addressed to the editor of The Dispatch. On the envelope was inscribed: "This contains a copy of the New York Times delivered by Captain St. Clair Streett, U. S. army, N. Y. to Nome, Alaska, aero expedition." It was signed by the editor of the New York Times.

Obviously the package had changed hands before the flight started.

The flight from New York to Erie was made in faster time than it took a telegraph message to be wired and delivered to the Exposition grounds. Almost an hour after the arrival of the aviators the manager of the Exposition grounds received a message from New York advising that the planes had departed at 12:30.

Famished and tired from their long flight, the trio was hurried to a luncheon prepared by a joint committee of Red Cross canteen workers, including Mrs Frederick C. Jarecki, Mrs. Theron R. Palmer, Mrs. Mason Mizener, the Misses Emma and Sylvia Russell and Mrs. Charles H. Strong.

Oil and gasoline were ready for the mechanics, but after cleaning the planes Lieutenant Nutt announced they would remain here over night to await word from Captain Streett. The planes will probably remain here today and the flight to Grand Rapids, Mich., the second stop, begun Saturday.

All machines were in perfect condition following the flight, Lieutenant Nutt said, and no time will be necessary for repairs. The planes are of the de Haviland type, which proved a great success throughout the war. They are equipped with Liberty motors and are capable of maintaining a speed of 120 miles an hour.

The flight is being made in the interest of establishing an aerial mail route to the northwest, with a possible aerial mail invasion of western Asia. Nome, the last stop in Alaska, is only a short distance from the coast of Asia.

Following the stop at Grand Rapids, Mich., the expedition plans to pursue this itinerary: Winona, Wis.; Fargo, N. D.; Portal, N. D.; Saskatoon, Sas.; Edmonton, Alberta; Jasper, Alberta; Prince George, B. C.; Hazelton, B. C.; Wrangel, Alaska; White Horse, Alaska; Dawson, Yukon; Fairbanks, Alaska; Ruby, Alaska, and Nome.

In addition to establishing an aerial route to the northwestern part of the American continent, one of the principal purposes of the flight is to photograph an important area in Alaska, which is comparatively inaccessible and has never been surveyed. The tract lies to the south of the Tanana river and is approximately 170 miles long and 65 miles wide.

Scranton, Pa., July 15—Having lost his way in a fog bank into which he flew soon after ascending at Mineola this afternoon, Captain St. Claire Streett, commander of the flight to Nome, Alaska, made a landing this afternoon at Elmhurst, eight miles east of this city. In landing the axle of the plane was broken, but Captain Streett and his mechanician were not injured. They expect to resume the flight at noon tomorrow.

Captain Streett described the fog as being extremely heavy and said that although they ascended over six thousand feet they were unable to escape it. Having lost their bearings he decided to descend. By a peculiar coincidence they landed on the same farm Lieutenant Kirkpatrick, one of their flying mates on the present trip, landed on last summer when he lost his way flying to this city.

Erie Daily Dispatch
July 16

To Grand Rapids

It rained in Erie for several days after the squadron landed. The landing field turned into a bog, and it was July 20, five days after departure from Mitchel Field, before it dried out enough for a takeoff. Grand Rapids, 300 miles away, was the second stop on the long journey north.

Crumrine in Plane No. 3 wanted to take off first so he could take some oblique photographs from the air. His plane started down the heavy turf but suddenly its wheel cut deep into the surface. He quickly cut his engine, but the momentum carried his plane another 100 feet forward. It finally bumped to a halt with one blade of the propeller sticking into the mud.

Luckily, the aircraft was not damaged, and the two crewmen were not hurt. But it was clear that no plane was going to get off the field in its present condition. A team of horses was employed to pull the plane back to firmer ground, and a heavy steam roller arrived to dry and firm up the surface. Even the roller got stuck in the mud.

By late afternoon it appeared the field was suitable for another try. There was 600 feet of rolled runway with a line of trees 40 feet high at the end. Crumrine was again going to try a takeoff so he could photograph the field from the air.

He made it almost to the end of the runway with his wheels clinging to the mud. It looked like he was going to head straight for the trees and a possible deadly crash. With all his effort, he pulled the nose of the plane straight up, and it became airborne, just clearing the trees by a foot, a very close call.

Once in the air, he unbuckled his seat belt to lean over the side to take his oblique photographs. Suddenly the plane was caught in a downdraft and Crumrine was suspended in midair. Sgt. Long, in the back seat, hauled back hard on the controls, and the plane rose quickly enough to catch the pilot and drop him back into his seat, another close call.

After the dangerous takeoff by Crumrine, Capt. Streett decided the squadron should wait one more day to let the field dry out thoroughly. By this time, the captain was beginning to wonder if his expedition would ever get to Nome.

The next morning, July 21, the three remaining planes took off without incident and headed over Lake Erie. They immediately hit a headwind, and each pilot worried about his gasoline supply. A forced landing in the frigid water was not a desirable option.

Streett's plane was getting low on fuel, but after two hours and 40 minutes he landed at Selfridge Field, an army airfield at Mt. Clemens, Mich. After gassing up, he took off for Grand Rapids, flying through thick weather and showers.

Crumrine had landed the day before at Roseswift Field in Grand Rapids. A local pilot went up in the air to guide him in. Three of Crumrine's sisters had traveled from Chicago to greet their brother, their first reunion in several years. The other two planes had overflown Selfridge Field and landed ahead of Streett.

When Streett landed he delivered a July 15 copy of the *New York Times* to the editor of the *Grand Rapids Herald*, the first newspaper ever delivered by air to the city.

Hundreds of citizens of Grand Rapids were waiting to greet the airmen, including members of the Grand Rapids Aero Club. After the planes were tied down and checked over, the eight air heroes were taken into town for a variety of entertainment. Crumrine was given a letter from a woman in Grand Rapids to deliver to her brother in Fairbanks. This must have been the first letter delivered by air into Alaska.

PLANES EXPECT TO REACH THIS CITY THURSDAY

Nome-Alaska Aircraft Have All Reached Grand Rapids, Mich., Today.

Grand Rapids, Mich., July 21.— Machine No. 1 arrived this afternoon. The planes bucked a strong head wind thruout the flight and were out of sight of land more than an hour crossing Lake Erie. Capt. Street plans to attempt the third jump to Winona, Minn., tomorrow.

Winona *Republican-Herald*, July 21.

VIEWS OF CRAFT ON WHICH ARMY FLYERS DEPEND TO PERFORM ALASKA TRICK

Herewith is shown on the ground and in flight the De Haviland 4-B plane to which the army is entrusting the success of its epochal "Polar Bear" flight from New York city to Nome, Alaska, and return, a distance of 8,690 miles. One of the four planes, with polar bears painted as insignia on the fuselage, arrived in Grand Rapids Tuesday evening. All are an improvement upon the old D. H.-4 used in the war and in the transcontinental trip and are equipped for all emergencies of a journey over unmapped and wild territory, even guns and ammunition being carried to kill game in case of a forced landing. Much of the flight will be at an altitude of 11,000 feet, due to the mountainous country traversed in the rockies and in Alaska. At these high altitudes the thinner air prevents the speed which the motor ordinarily will turn up. The man in the air dreads fire more than any other single risk and to minimize the Liberty motors used in this flight are equipped with an intake manifold stack. In case of a backfire from any of the cylinders which might ignite the gasoline in the carburetor the intake stack affords an outlet over the top of the engine for the flame.

The Grand Rapids Herald

Nutt's plane ready for a night's rest at Grand Rapids. RAA

Hangar at the Roseswift Airport at Grand Rapids. RAA

The expedition's hosts at Grand Rapids, Mich. Seated from left: Nutt, Nelson, Henriques, Kirkpatrick and Crumrine. Standing on right, English and Long. RAA

BLAZERS OF TRAIL TO ALAKSA LEAVE WITH NO TROUBLE

Conditions Ideal as Polar Bears Hop Off for Winona, Minn.

CROSS LAKE MICHIGAN

Sisters of Lieut. Crumrine in Smiling Though Tearful Farewell.

All four Polar Bear army airplanes bound from New York to Nome, Alaska, hopped off together from Grand Rapids at 11:30 a. m. Thursday, heading for the next scheduled stop, Winona, Minn., 310 miles away across Lake Michigan.

Plane No. 4 was first to take the air from the Rosewift aviation field. Ross Kirkpatrick gave it the throttle at prompt 11:30 and 15 seconds later he was off the ground. Lieut. C. W. Nutt followed a minute later in Plane No. 3, while Lieut. C. E. Crumrine got off in 30 seconds after No. 2, his three sisters waving him a smiling though tearful farewell.

To Cross Big Lake.

Capt. St. Clair Street in Plane No. 1 hopped off at 11:34. The first three machines circled the field several times, gaining altitude, and headed for the west as soon as Capt. Street mounted the air. They did not go over Grand Rapids, but set their course directly for Grand Haven. They were out of sight within five minutes after they started.

"We expect to take a straight path across Lake Michigan from Grand Haven, Mich., to Port Washington, Wis., about 20 miles north of Milwaukee," said Capt. Street as he said goodby. "We will cross the entire state of Wisconsin to Winona which is on the border of Minnesota and Wisconsin.

"I understand this is the first time land planes have ventured to cross Lake Michigan, but I anticipate not the slightest difficulty."

Weather Is Ideal.

The planes were favored by ideal weather in leaving Grand Rapids. They had a mild east wind behind them and the sky was clear save for a few hazy summer clouds.

The aviators expected to reach Winona before 3 o'clock.

Pass Grand Haven at Noon.

Grand Haven, July 22.—The four Polar Bear flyers passed over this city at 12 o'clock Thursday, flying at high altitude. All four planes were together. They were heading straight west out over Lake Michigan.

Upper picture, at left, shows Lieut. C. E. Crumrine, plucky aviator on the long flight from New York to Nome, Alaska, and his mechanician, Sergt. James B. Long who performed a daring fete when, about to land, he crawled back to the tail of the De Haviland to steady the course of the plane to the ground.

Lower picture shows part of the crowd which greeted the birdmen. The crowd was not large at the instant of the landing of the plane, but the news that the Polar Bear had arrived spread quickly and in a short time there were many visitors on the field. The flyers immediately got busy cleaning up the plane and though they arrived at about 5:45 they did not put the plane in the hangar until 8 p. m. Lieut. Crumrine and Sergt. Long slept late Wednesday morning.

Crumrine Is First to Reach Grand Rapids on New York-Nome Flight

Dipping gracefully to earth, with an olive drab clad mechanic poised on its tail, Polar Bear plane No. 3, piloted by Lieut. C. E. Crumrine, ended the second lap of its long flight from New York to Nome, Alaska, at Rosewift airport at 5:43 Tuesday afternoon, just three hours and 58 minutes after leaving Erie, Pa., 300 miles away. The De Haviland first winged its way over the field, searching the best spot to land, and Arthur Rosenthal, president of the local company, went up with "Steve" Goodrich as pilot in a Rosewift plane to demonstrate a landing. The Polar Bear then came gently to earth with Sergt. James D. Long back on the fuselage for a balance.

Lieut. Crumrine left Erie at 1:45 Tuesday afternoon, flying directly across Lake Erie on a course which brought him into Michigan slightly west of Detroit. He then flew straight for Grand Rapids, passing a few miles north of Lansing and picking up the line of the Grand river from there to his destination. His speed during most of the trip was 90 miles an hour, and his altitude 3,000 feet. Visibility was good all the way until within 10 miles of Grand Rapids when, Lieut. Crumrine says, the atmosphere became rather hazy. Going was easy, despite a slight head wind throughout the journey. This was in contrast to the first lap of the trip in which fog and rain made flying difficult and caused the accident to Capt. St. Clair Street's machine which delayed the flyers at Erie.

Difficulty in Starting.

Lieut. Crumrine says the principal difficulty which prevented the start from Erie was that two days of rain made the field so soggy that the four planes were bogged and could not get into the air. Attempting to get away at 9:15 Tuesday morning Lieut. Crumrine managed to get his plane a few feet off the ground, but there was insufficient momentum and the De Haviland nosed into the earth, breaking a shock absorber casing on the landing gear and striking so hard that stowage in the box behind the rear cockpit smashed through the cover. Spending the rest of the morning in repairing this damage Lieut. Crumrine finally was ready for another trial and with the aid of a team of horses which dragged the plane to a strip of dried ground (Continued on Fifth Page.)

The Grand Rapids Herald

To Winona and Minneapolis

The next stop would be the Mississippi River town of Winona, Minnesota, 310 miles to the west. The next morning, July 22, a large crowd was again on hand to say goodbye.

Capt. Streett took off first with the others leaving at 30 second intervals. They climbed to 2,000 feet and got into formation then set a course of 284 degrees for Winona, with an east wind blowing at 15 m.p.h. After 20 minutes they flew above Grand Haven, Michigan, on the shores of Lake Michigan. A ground mist limited visibility to a 10-mile radius.

It was dangerous to fly over such a large expanse of water as Lake Michigan with a fixed wheel plane, so as they approached the lake they reached an altitude of 7,000 feet. In case of motor trouble, this would give the pilot a longer distance to glide if he were forced to land on the water. This was the first time a land plane had flown over Lake Michigan.

Streett again was having problems. As he approached the west shore of the lake, he noticed that his fuel gauge showed a rapid loss of pressure. He was too far from a safe landing to switch to his reserve tank. With Henriques taking the controls, Streett pulled out a hand pump from beneath his seat, attached it to the fuel line, and pumped frantically to keep the fuel flowing. When Winona was sighted, he took back the controls, switched to his reserve tank and landed safely. When Sgt. Henriques examined the line afterwards, he found a small particle of dirt had jammed into the pressure relief valve.

Winona is nestled in a valley between hills sharply rising to an elevation of 1,000 feet. The valley runs northwest to southeast, so the prevailing winds are always in one of these directions. The aviator must determine, before he lands his plane, the direction of the wind and, if possible, head directly into it as his plane glides down the field. And if the field is small, it is very important to notice the direction of the wind from smoke drift on the ground, then head into the wind and permit it to retard the speed of the plane upon landing.

The citizens of Winona rushed to greet the crews at Biesanz Field and insisted they stay for a luncheon.

However, it was decided to fly all the planes to Minneapolis the same day so the axle on Streett's plane, damaged at Erie, could be repaired properly. The flight to Minneapolis would take only a little over an hour, and they were ready to leave after a quick dinner at the Schlitz Hotel in Winona.

At 6 p.m., with the people of Winona watching, the squadron took off and an hour later was joined by a plane that escorted them to a large landing field four miles south of the Twin Cities. The field was one of the best they would land on and had adequate facilities for fuel and mechanical repairs.

The planes were again met by an enthusiastic crowd, and the crewmen were featured in a parade through downtown Minneapolis and at a dinner at the Minneapolis Athletic Club hosted by the local Aero Club.

THE WINONA REPUBLICAN-HERALD,

Winona Republican-Herald, July 22

ARMY PLANES FLY TO MINNEAPOLIS IN 45 MINUTES LATE ON THURSDAY AFTERNOON

Winona Reception Liked—Party Plans to Spend Whole Day in This City on Return.

VOYAGERS TO FAR NORTH TO VISIT UNKNOWN WILDS IN WEST CANADA

Circling the air like mighty birds, glimmering in the rays of the setting sun like vultures of silver, the four big army planes bound for Alaska, rose off Biesanz Field at 6 p. m. Thursday to fly to Minneapolis. Army preciseness prevailed and with one accord the big propellers were "flopped" and the powerful engines began their incessant humming. "By the numbers" the planes took off and rose gracefully and beautifully over the waving fields of grain and corn. One after the other they circled over the field until all were in the air and then, in fleet formation, started up the river, following Capt. St. Clair, in plane No. 1 which had already reached Fountain City while the other ships were taking off.

Many Winonans witnessed the departure.

Flight Short

The flight to Minneapolis took less than 45 minutes and the landing was successful and without mishap. The trip to the Mill City had not been planned but was found necessary, it is stated, in order to replace in position the hanging of one of the wheels on Capt. Street's plane. Today the expedition continued on its way to Fargo, N. D., a jump of about 300 miles.

"We certainly would enjoy visiting at Winona, now that we are here," said Capt. Street to the local committee on the flying field Thursday afternoon, "but we must have my machine put back in shape before we get further west. I can assure you, however, that on our return trip next fall, it may be possible for us to stay over a day at Winona. Your kindness and hospitality is greatly appreciated by all of us."

Grand Rapids Field Muddy

"We had a miserable time on the small muddy field at Grand Rapids and have lost valuable time. Your field here is splendid but ought to be somewhat larger."

The eight visitors were provided with dinner at the Schlitz hotel at 5 o'clock and then hurried back to the field where the planes were in readiness.

Especially equipped for the long flight, the planes each carry 117 gallons of gasoline and 12 gallons of oil. Spectators at the Winona field were amazed at the great carrying capacity of the big machines. All are De-Haviland 4-B Liberty machines.

Canadian Helps

An officer of the Canadian Air Service assisted Capt. Howard T. Douglas in laying out the route they are traversing and the Canadian Weather Bureau will co-operate with the American Weather Bureau in furnishing the aviators with daily weather reports.

In addition to establishing an aerial route to the northwestern part of the American continent, one of the principal purposes of the flight is to photograph an important area in that territory which is comparatively inaccessible and has never been surveyed. The tract lies to the south of the Tanana River and is approximately 170 miles long and 65 miles wide.

Lieuts. Nelson and Nutt, two of the flight officers have had special courses of training at the Air Service School of Aerial Photography at Langley Field near Hampton, Va.

Now Move North

Grand Rapids, Mich., marked the turning point where the airplane were pointed northward toward Nome. All is expected well along the route until the fliers reach Jasper, Alberta, Can. There the most difficult part of the flight begins. The Canadian Rockies are encountered soon after leaving Jasper and are known to be a part of the most rugged and inaccessible region in the northwestern part of the North American continent. Speed will be reduced from that point on and the planes will probably only make one jump a day or 250 miles of flying.

In flying over the country the pilots will have to rely entirely on their compasses, and their ability as aerial navigators will have a thoro test. The success of the expedition is dependent largely on the performance of the Liberty motor with which each plane is equipped.

Planes Well Equipped

Each plane carries mosquito helmets, a concentrated supply of food, as well as revolvers, shotguns, fishing tackle, etc., for emergency. Every precaution has been taken to guard against any trouble whatsoever, and it is believed that the planes will complete the trip, encountering only minor troubles which will not call for forced landings.

On reaching Nome, Alaska, the expedition will make a 100-mile flight to Cape Prince of Wales, at which point it will be approximately 50 miles from the continent of Asia.

The Flights

The 9,000 mile route of the fliers with the distance between each stopping point is as follows:

New York (Mitchell Field) to Erie, Pa., 350 miles; Erie to Grand Rapids, Mich., 300 miles; Grand Rapids to Winona, Minn., 510 miles; Winona to Fargo, N. D., 330 miles; Fargo to Portal, N. D., 290 miles; Portal to Saskatoon, Sask., Canada, 280 miles;

Saskatoon to Edmonton, Alberta, 300 miles; Edmonton to Jasper, Alberta, 200 miles; Jasper to Prince George, B. C., 300 miles; Prince George to Hazelton, B. C., 220 miles; Hazelton to Wrangell, Alaska, 310 miles; Wrangell to White Horse, Yukon, 300 miles; White Horse to Dawson, Yukon, 250 miles; Dawson to Fairbanks, 275 miles; Fairbanks to Ruby, 240 miles; Ruby to Nome, 300 miles.

According to Capt. Street the fliers had planned on stopping in Minneapolis on their return trip from Alaska but with their plans changed, they will make a stop-over at Winona next September.

MADISON WANTS ARMY AVIATORS

Mrs. H. L. Potter, Aviatrix, Asks Visit from Capt. Street's Party.

"Won't you and your aviator boys come over to Madison and visit us?"

A sweet voice over long distance phone put this query to Capt. St. Clair Street Thursday afternoon.

"This is Mrs. H. L. Potter at Madison," the voice continued.

"I am very sorry, Mrs. Potter, but it is impossible for us to come to Madison at this time. However, when we return next fall, it may be possible for us to stop briefly at your city. We fly direct to Minneapolis from Winona and will leave in a few hours," the aviation captain answered.

Mrs. Potter is the aviatrix who came to Winona last August and took up a number of passengers at the Neville Field. A very clever exhibition of stunt flying was performed over the city on a Sunday afternoon by her pilot. A trip to neighboring towns with the machine and a generous shower of handbills brot thousands of people to Winona for the exhibition.

PLANES BRING NEW YORK TIMES

Paper Sent From Editor to Republican-Herald Delivered.

"This envelope contains a copy of The New York Times delivered by Capt. St. Clair Street, U. S. Army, New York to Nome, Alaska, Aero Expedition.—Editor, The New York Times."

This is the inscription on a large envelope addressed to the editor of The Republican-Herald and delivered at Biesanz Field by Capt. Street, Thursday, a few minutes after the big planes had alighted. It contained a well preserved copy of the New York Times, issue of Thursday, July 15.

The New York daily which had made the long trip of nearly 1,000 miles by air over mountains, rivers and over Lake Erie and the widest part of Lake Michigan finds many interested readers at The Republican-Herald office.

MANY FLYERS ARE INVITED

Fail to Meet Army Aviators During Thursday Visit, However.

Invitations to come to Winona and meet the army fliers of the Alaskan expedition were sent to aviators in all parts of the Northwest yesterday by Charles Biesanz, owner of the landing field, M-13. It was expected that several fliers could arrange to come to Winona and meet the fleet of army machines down the river and lead them into Winona.

A flier with headquarters at Galesville who performed for those at the Kiwanis picnic this week promised his attendance. It was reported, also, that Herbert Riebe would come to Winona but over long distance telephone he stated that would be impossible.

Messages were sent also to fliers at La Crosse and the Twin Cities.

An aerial view of Winona, Minnesota, on the Mississippi River. RAA

Aerial view of Biesanz Field at Winona, Minnesota. Notice the shadow of one of the DH-4s in the bottom center of the photo. RAA

STEERING GEAR TROUBLE STOPS ALASKA PLANES

Repairs Are Made Quickly in Minneapolis on Friday, However—Start Today.

Minneapolis, July 24.—Trouble with a damaged steering gear prevented the scheduled hop-off from Minneapolis yesterday noon of the four United States army airplanes of the New York to Nome, Alaska, expedition. The squadron will take off from the Speedway flying field at 9:30 this morning for Fargo, N. D., the necessary repairs to the damaged machine having been made late yesterday, Capt. St. Clair Street, flight commander, announced last night.

Members of the Minneapolis Aero club welcomed the change in plans and entertained the eight pilots and mechanics of the squadron at the Minneapolis club and the Minneapolis Athletic club at dinner last night. The officers of the club, Rufus Rand, Jr., Perry Williams, W. F. Brooks and Paul Goldsworthy, were with the visiting fliers at the Speedway field all yesterday afternoon, inspecting the planes and discussing future of Minneapolis as an airplane traffic center.

Postmaster Purdy was also at the field and accompanied by Capt. Street inspected the government hangars being constructed for use of mail airplanes. Progress made on the work brought the prediction that the hangars would be ready for use by the mail service Aug. 1. The field itself was declared to be one of the best in the West by Capt. Street.

When the four planes of the squadron landed in Minneapolis at 7:20 Thursday night, they had covered 1,080 miles of their itinerary to Alaska and return, which is expected to total more than 9,000 miles. They left Mitchell flying field at Mineola, Long Island, July 15, making landings at Scranton and Erie, Pa.; Grand Rapids, Mich., and Winona, Minn., before their arrival here.

Members of the group experienced only one real thrill during the journey here, they said. That was their flight over Lake Michigan at its widest point when they were out of sight of land for nearly an hour. It is believed their flight was the first made across the lake in land machines. They will cross the Canadian border at Portal, N. D., the second scheduled landing point after leaving Minneapolis this morning. A large part of the trip will be made over Canadian territory, arrangements having been made with the Dominion government.

The Nome, Alaska, objective of the expedition is expected to be reached by August 10. Photographic and exploring work will be undertaken by the planes during the ensuing 30 days and the return trip to New York will be started by September 20, in time to escape the early Alaskan snows.

Aerial views of the landing field and the surrounding speedway at Minneapolis, Minnesota. RAA

Winona Republican-Herald
July 24

To Fargo

For the first time on the trip a weather forecast kept the planes on the ground for two days in Minneapolis. Severe storms had been reported over Fargo, North Dakota, the next stop on the flight. The crew spent its time maintaining the aircraft for the most dangerous part of the trip: the almost 1,400 miles through the Canadian providences and over the high, rugged Rocky Mountains.

On July 24, at 11:47 a.m., the squadron took off for Fargo, 225 miles to the west. A 10-m.p.h. wind blew across the flight line. As Captain Streett stated in his journal: "Ten minutes of flying through clouds brought us suddenly out into a beautiful, clear sky. For the first time we feasted our eyes upon the famous clear landscapes of the West.

"From our altitude of 5,000 feet we could see the horizon, 40 or 50 miles away, all around us. Never had I flown through an atmosphere so pure and clean. Innumerable small lakes dotted the lovely landscape. Smiling and well-kept farms occupied every foot of dry land."

A favorable wind helped the DH-4s to cruise along at just over 100 m.p.h. They arrived in Fargo at 1:15 p.m., two hours and 24 minutes after leaving Minneapolis, and landed at the A.C. Field, with Fitzpatrick coming in first. Another big crowd was on hand to greet the planes, and a public luncheon was offered. But Streett had his crews wash down the planes, refuel them and make minor adjustments instead, so they all ate cold sandwiches. Streett was busy painting the edges of his plane, which had taken a beating on the first leg to Erie days ago.

The night was spent in Fargo for a good rest before the next leg into Canada.

Aerial view of Fargo, North Dakota. RAA

ARMY PLANES REACH FARGO FIVE DAYS LATE

Army airplanes due in Fargo July 19, left Minneapolis this morning at 10:35 this morning, headed for Fargo, and were due to land on the A. C. field early this afternoon.

Captain St. Clair Street is commanding the expedition. Lieut. Clifford C. Nutt, second in command; and Lieutenants Kirkpatrick, Nelson and Crumline are each in command of a plane.

The expedition left New York on July 15, and were due to reach Fargo inside of four days. They ran into stormy weather around Erie, Pa., their first stop, and were delayed there several days. From Erie, they jumped off for Grand Rapids, and from Grand Rapids to Winona, Minn. From Winona they flew to Minneapolis instead of to Fargo, their next scheduled stop, stopping in Minneapolis for needed repairs, and remaining there nearly two days.

Supplies, including repairs, gasoline and oil, have been on the landing field north of the city for two days in readiness for their arrival. Two men from the Fargo police station and one man from the recruiting office are detailed as guards for the planes during their stay in Fargo.

They will leave Fargo for Portal, N. D., then jumping over the Canadian border on the longest stretch of their flight to Nome, Alaska, on the Bering strait.

Weather Reports.

Elaborate plans were made by the United States weather bureau for making special weather reports accessible to flyers along the entire route. In addition the commanding officer of the expedition is receiving special local weather reports. The Canadian government weather bureau promised to co-operate in the undertaking by furnishing daily weather forecasts.

The maps for the expedition were carefully arranged and prepared by the Information Group of the United States Army Air Service. Much of the territory over which the flyers are passing has never been adequately mapped nor photographed. The expedition is expected to furnish accurate data for mapping some of the sections of Alaska hitherto inaccessible.

Alaskan Hardships Overcome.

"There are many advantages that will accrue from this expedition," says a statement from the War department in which the plans for the expedition were described. "One in particular will be the fact that following this effort both commercial and small aircraft may utilize this route so that the scenic wonders and natural resources and the many advantages of Alaska, which have hitherto been forbidden to all but to courageous pioneers who were willing to cope with the hardships incidental to such a trip, will in the future be obtained with a few days' travel in luxury and comfort.

"Where the mail at present from the interior of Alaska is 30 days or more in reaching the United States it will become a matter of a few days to bring this mail from the very heart of Alaska to the very heart of the United States. Ranchmen and others along the line of the route have co-operated magnificently with those in charge of the expedition and are awake to the tremendous possibilities and advantages to be derived from contact between their small local communities and the great metropolitan centers of the country. A successful culmination of this expedition will mean the closest sort of co-operation between the Air Board of Canada and the Army Air Service to the end that the North American continent may be served by commercial aircraft from one end to the other.

To Photograph Inaccessible Alaska.

"A second reason which indicates the utility of this expedition is the co-operation of the Army Air Service with the Engineering corps and the Geological Survey for the purpose of photographing inaccessible areas in Alaska, which have heretofore not been mapped. One area in particular, which the Geological survey especially desires to have photographed from the air comprises 3,500 square miles lying north of the sixty-sixth parallel, between Fort Hamlin and Circle. This area includes the upper Yukon flats, and is a district which can only be surveyed by ground methods with extreme difficulty. Representatives of the United geological survey have estimated that it would cost $10,000 and would take one surveying party at least three seasons, which would mean three years to accomplish this work by the present ground methods. It would then, only be partially accurate.

"Allowing for a 50 per cent overlap of the photographs from the air, this area can be photographed from one airplane in 10 hours of flying, or approximately three days' time, at a cost of about $1,500 and the data assembled from such a photograph would be more accurate than could be obtained from the ground in the short time available each year.

"Cameras are being used by the expedition in Alaska for taking ground views at the stops and obliques and vertical views while en route. In addition cameras and films are provided for the photographic mapping of the area north of the parallel 66 degrees, which includes the Yukon river where it crosses the parallel between Circle and Fort Hamlin. The photographic phase of the expedition will utilize Fairbanks, Alaska, as a base of operation for all major repairs to airplanes for the Alaskan end of the flight.

This article appeared in *The Fargo Forum*, July 24, 1920. It states that two Fargo policemen and a military recruiting officer will guard the planes during their stay in the city.

ARMY PLANES TAKE OFF FOR NOME AFTER A STOP AT FARGO

Squadron Leaves Fargo At 9:30 Sunday, Now Well Into Canada

Portal, N. D., July 26.—Speeding up their flying planes, the four army airplanes on a flight from Mineola, L. I., to Nome, Alaska, departed from here at 10 o'clock today, on their way through northwestern Canada. Saskatoon is the first scheduled stopping place in the Dominion.

With just a light breeze wafting the scent of sweet clover and newly cut hay from the A. C. fields, to mingle with the scent of gasoline and oil from staccato explosions from the Ford Liberty motors of the big army airplanes, army aviators bound for Nome, Alaska, on the Bering strait hopped off from Fargo for Portal, N. D., at promptly 9:30 o'clock yesterday morning. They will stop in Fargo on their return flight probably some time in September.

The machines arrived in Fargo at 1:15 on Saturday afternoon, two hours and 40 minutes after leaving Minneapolis. Circling over Fargo in their search for the "T" marked landing field, they finally swooped down upon the field, plane No. 4 in command of Lieut. Ross C. Kirkpatrick, alighting first.

They reported almost ideal flying conditions on the flight from Minneapolis to Fargo, although the weather at the altitude at which they were travelling, 4,000 feet, was slightly chilly.

Captain Street

Capt. St. Clair Street, in command of the expedition, was busy slapping green and black paint on scuffed edges of his plane, No. 1, when a Forum representative hove in sight. Slight, small, but wiry looking, he looked exceedingly capable. During the war he was officer in charge of training at the largest overseas aerial training camp, spending 18 months in overseas service.

Other members of the expedition were lazily stretcher in the shade of the wing of his big plane, munching huge cheese sandwiches, and making a large basket of "eats" disappear with almost incredible rapidity. Grimy from the dust, clad in khaki overalls, spattered with oil and grease, they were in the best of humor and ventured much more news about the trip than Captain Street himself seemed to want to tell.

Lieutenant Kirkpatrick, detailed as "Information Officer for the Press," by Captain Street, explained that Captain Street was supposed to have run into a heavy hail storm outside of Erie, Pa., which was responsible for the scuffed condition of his plane, and also responsible for the condition of Sergeant Henriques, who was knocked unconscious by the heavy hail stones and had not, as yet, recovered. Sergeant Henriques, was a "Lime" from England, and otherwise very efficient, he said. The sergeant, busy with a banana, simply grinned.

Cornfield Landing

Another story in circulation about the bruised condition of the plane, which Lieutenant Kirkpatrick explained was a dark secret, and might be substantiated by asking the captain, was that Captain Street had mistaken a cornfield outside of Erie for the landing field.

At this point, Lieutenant Crumrine, in command of plane No. 3, abandoned his sandwich long enough to request that if anything be put in the paper at all about the expedition, it be carefully explained that Lieutenant Kirkpatrick was born in a castle near Dublin, Ireland.

Overseas Planes.

The airplanes used in the flight were huge affairs, weighing 4,250 lbs., and having 400 horsepower. They are four times as large as the ordinary Curtiss plane, and were known as the DeHaviland Army 4-B type. The motors used in them were the Henry Ford Liberty motor. Planes similar to these were used overseas during the war.

In each plane there was room for two passengers, the pilot and the observer. They carried 117 gallons of gasoline and 12 gallons of oil, providing them with a cruising radius of from four and a half to five hours. Painted on the side of the plane, or the fuselage, was the insignia of the expedition, the head of a polar bear.

This article appeared in the *Forum* on July 26. In it Sgt. Henriques is reported to be from England. Other sources state that he was originally from Canada or Australia. Crumrine jokingly told the press Kirkpatrick's birthplace was Dublin, Ireland. These articles give a clear picture as to the excitement and importance placed on this expedition to open up the air spaces of the Northwest and Alaska.

ARMY FLYERS MAPPING AIR LINE TO ASIA; WILL SURVEY ALASKAN WASTES, OPEN FROZEN NORTH TO CIVILIZATION.

Left to right: Capt. St. Clair Street, commanding the expedition; Lieut. Clifford C. Nutt, second in command; Lieuts. Kirkpatrick, Nelson and Crumline, each in command of a plane.

ARMY PLANES STOP AT FARGO

The *Fargo Forum*, July 26

To Portal

Portal, North Dakota, on the Saskatchewan border would be the final stop before flying into Canada. At 9:30 a.m. on July 25, the planes took off from Fargo for the final 290-mile leg in the United States. All went well until landing three hours and 10 minutes later.

At 1 p.m., the planes circled the field, just to the northwest and across the border from the small town of Portal, to look for obstructions such as ditches, fences or stumps. Kirkpatrick came in first and landed perfectly, but cut his tires badly on glass that was strewn along the runway. Later it was discovered that the area had been used as the town dump.

Crumrine and Streett landed without incident, but Nutt rolled over an inconspicuous bump and broke off his tail skid. The tires were repaired by binding them securely with electrician's tape. The skid proved to be a much more difficult repair. Sgt. English went to a local garage where he found an old Ford axle, a piece of which was welded on to make a new skid.

The repairs took till 8 p.m., so another night was spent before takeoff.

A crowd, seen at the upper right in the photograph, watches the landings near Portal. The outline of one plane can be seen just to the right of center. The landing field is presumed to be in the middle, running from top to bottom at a slight angle in the photo. RAA

Portal, North Dakota, was just a small village on the Saskatchewan border.
RAA

THE STAR GOES HOME

American Flyers Jump From Portal Without Incident

AVERAGE SEVENTY MILES AN HOUR AGAINST WIND OF FORTY MILES—McCLELLAND TAKES LADY PASSENGER UP IN THE AIR TO MEET THEM

At 12:57 today the first of the four United States Army airplanes landed at the McClelland aerodrome, followed in quick succession by its three companions. The planes had left Portal, North Dakota, at 9:05 this morning (Saskatoon time) and the average ground speed maintained throughout the "jump" was 70 miles an hour.

The total flying time out of New York is now 15 hours. The machines left Mineola, Long Island, on Thursday, July 15, but were delayed seven days owing to bad weather.

"We had a rather strong head wind," said Capt. St. Clair Street, commander of the expedition, "of between 35 and 40 miles an hour. In fact, we have had head winds all the way from Mineola, with the single exception of the jump from Fargo to Portal yesterday."

GIVEN REAL RECEPTION

Saskatoon accorded the aviators a real reception. Lieut. H. R. McClelland, the head aviator, had marked his landing field with the word "Welcome," written with big strips of cheese cloth pegged to the ground.

At 12:35 McClelland took off on a passenger-carrying flight, with Mrs. A. L. Lynd as his passenger. It was barely well into the air before he apparently caught sight of Capt. Street's plane looming up from the southeast. McClelland, varying from his aerial passenger-carrying route, headed straight into the southwest and kept that course for about ten minutes. It was not until McClelland turned and headed straight back for the drome that the keen eyes of the waiting crowd, which stood around the drome, saw a faint black speck in the sky over McClelland's place. Within a few minutes the other three planes were seen.

McClelland made a quick landing on Capt. Street, who was in the lead, made a landing after circling the hangars twice. The other machines, which had been circling like great buzzards, came to earth one by one and were lined up in front of the McClelland hangars.

The machines are all painted a dark khaki color, and when seen from the ground appear to be almost black. They carry the star of the American air force, and on the tail a black wolf's head in a circle.

Their wingspan is slightly less than that of the Curtiss plane than McClelland, but the machines are much higher and heavier, particularly the bodies. Three are twelve-cylinder Liberty type, developing 400 horsepower each. They have an amazing ground while on the air and a noise like an electric locomotive or traction engine while idling on the ground.

FLYERS MUCH PLEASED

Capt. Street was simply pleased by the reception accorded him. The aviators were invited to lunch by Mayor Young, but were forced to decline. Capt. Street said it was an invariable rule to "put the ships in shape" before leaving them. Each motor is carefully washed and inspected and necessary adjustments are made, before the aviators turn the plane over to the care of a watchman.

The motors were brand new when they started on this trip, and are being "nursed" as new motors must be.

"In the eastern states," said Capt. Street, "the people have come to look upon us aviators as a nuisance like a grasshopper or a June bug. But here we have been welcomed royally."

The aviators will be the guests of the city until they "take off" for Edmonton at 9.30 tomorrow morning.

Each plane was supplied with 25 gallons of gasoline and 12 gallons of lubricating oil by the Imperial Oil Co.

Capt. Street presented the news editor of The Star with an envelope containing a copy of the New York Times of Thursday, July 15, in which had been placed in his care by a representative of that newspaper on that date. The Times contained the following account of the plans for the expedition:

The war department announced late yesterday that all arrangements for the New York to Nome, Alaska, and return army flight had been completed and that, unless bad weather or some unforeseen circumstances prevent four De-Havilland 4-B Liberty airplanes will leave Mitchel Field, Garden City, at 10 o'clock this morning on the start of the 9,000-mile flight. Captain Howard T. Douglas, who has gone over the proposed route, locating landing fields and placing supplies at proper points, has reported that everything along the line of flight is ready. It has been estimated that the trip to Nome and return will take forty-five days.

The route of the Alaskan Flying Expedition will be:

New York (Mitchel Field) to Erie, Pa. 350 miles; Erie to Grand Rapids, Mich. 300 miles; Grand Rapids to Winona 310 miles; Winona to Fargo, N.D. 320 miles; Fargo to Portal, N.D. 290 miles; Portal to Saskatoon, Sask. Canada 290 miles; Saskatoon to Edmonton, Alberta, 300 miles; Edmonton to Jasper, Alberta, 200 miles; Jasper to Prince George, B.C. 200 miles; Prince George to Hazelton, B.C. 320 miles; Hazelton to Wrangell, Alaska, 210 miles; Wrangell to White Horse, Yukon, 310 miles; White Horse to Dawson, Yukon, 250 miles; Dawson to Fairbanks, 250

miles; Fairbanks to Ruby, 240 miles; Ruby to Nome, 300 miles.

On reaching Nome the expedition will make a 160-mile flight to Cape Prince of Wales at which point it will be approximately fifty miles from the continent of Asia.

This is the personnel of the expedition:

Plane 1—Captain St. Clair Street, pilot and commanding officer of the expedition, Sergeant Edmond Henriques, observer and mechanic.

Plane 2—First Lieutenant Clifford C. Nutt, second in command, pilot, Second Lieutenant Eric H. Nelson, engineering officer, pilot.

Plane 3—Second Lieutenant C. H. Crumrine, photographic officer, pilot and observer.

Plane 4—Second Lieutenant Ross Kirkpatrick, information officer and pilot, M. E. Sergeant Joseph E. English, mechanic and observer.

SPECIALLY EQUIPPED

Especially equipped for the long flight, the planes will carry 117 gallons of gasoline and 12 gallons of oil. An officer of the Canadian Air Service assisted Captain Douglas in laying out the route, and the Canadian Weather Bureau will co-operate with the American Weather Bureau in furnishing the aviators with daily weather reports.

In addition to establishing an aerial route to the northwestern part of the American continent, one of the principal purposes of the flight is to photograph an important area in that territory which is comparatively inaccessible and has never been surveyed. The tract lies to the south of the Tanana River and is approximately 170 miles long and 45 miles wide.

Lieutenants Nelson and Nutt, the two flight officers, have had special course of training at the Air Service School of Aerial Photography at Langley Field, near Hampton, Va.

Grand Rapids, Mich. marks the turning point where airplanes will be turned southward toward Nome, and all is expected to be well along the route until the fliers reach Jasper, Alberta, Canada. Here the most difficult and dangerous part of the flight begins. The Canadian Rockies are encountered soon after leaving Jasper and are known to be a part of the most rugged and inaccessible region in the northwest part of the North American continent. Speed will be reduced from this point on and the planes will probably only make one jump per day, or 250 miles of flying.

In flying over the country the pilots will have to rely entirely on their compasses and their ability as aerial navigators will have a thorough test. The success of the expedition is dependent largely on the performance of the Liberty motor with which each plane is equipped.

Each plane will carry mosquito helmets, a concentrated supply of food, tackle, etc. for emergency. Every pilot as well as revolvers, shotguns, fishing caution has been taken to guard against any trouble whatsoever, and it is believed that the planes will complete the trip, encountering only minor troubles, which will not call for forced landings.

SASKATOON *DAILY STAR*, JULY 25.

Nutt's plane was jacked up so a new tail skid could be attached. This photograph gives the reader a good view of the Black Wolf Squadron insignia. RAA

-40-

 *To Saskatoon*

On the morning of July 26, the squadron took off from the North Portal field and proceeded to Saskatoon, 280 miles to the northwest. At 5,000 feet, the sky was clear, and the flat farmland of Saskatchewan stretched out before the planes. They used the Canadian Pacific Railroad tracks to set their compass headings. They flew over Tyvan, Regina, Last Mountain Lake and finally Saskatoon.

At 1 p.m. the first plane landed at Lt. H.S. McClelland's airfield. McClelland had marked the field with the word "WELCOME," written with a big cheese-cloth pegged to the ground, and had gone up in the air to guide them in.

Mayor Young and members of the city council and Rotary Club were there to meet the crewmen. The mayor gave the official welcome: "Captain Street, and members of the Alaska expedition, on behalf of the present company and the citizens of Saskatoon, I take the opportunity to extend to you a very cordial official welcome to this city. We are very pleased that your government picked out this city as a landing place, and hope that everything has been to your liking. You have made history for this city and you are still making it. We wish you every success on your expedition and hope that every member of your party will come through your venture without mishap."

After the planes were serviced, the crew was taken to the King George Hotel, where a sumptuous banquet was held in honor of the expedition. Afterward the fliers were driven around the city and then taken to the Saskatoon Club for another official welcome. The Great War Veterans Band was brought in and played "The Star Spangled Banner" and "God Save The King." The mayor of Vancouver, British Columbia, gave a speech wishing the fliers success on their flight into his province.

Finally, it was off to bed so they could be ready for their next leg to Edmonton, Alberta, the next morning.

The *Saskatoon Phoenix*
July 27

SASKATOON GIVES WELCOME TO AMERICAN AVIATORS ON ARRIVAL AT LOCAL DROME

Four Birdmen en Route From Mineola to Nome Land at Lieut. McClelland's Air Harbor, Are Dined by City Fathers and Rotary Club Last Night

"Captain Street, and members of the Alaska expedition, on behalf of the present company and the citizens of Saskatoon, I take this opportunity to extend to you a very cordial official welcome to this city. We are very pleased that your government picked out this city as a landing place, and hope that everything has been to your liking. You have made history for this city and you are still making it. We wish you every success on your expedition and hope that every member of your party will come through your venture without mishap."

With these words Mayor Young gave an official welcome to the members of the American army flying expedition, who arrived in the city yesterday, at the Saskatoon club last night.

At one o'clock yesterday afternoon the first plane of the American expedition landed at the McClelland airdrome and was closely followed by its three companions. The four planes under the command of Captain St. Clair Street, are flying from Mineola, N.Y., to Nome, Alaska, and left Portal at nine o'clock yesterday morning, completing the 280 miles in a little less than four hours.

Lieut. McClelland, at whose airdrome the four American planes landed, had marked his landing-field with the word "Welcome" written with a big strip of cheese-cloth pegged to the ground.

Are Entertained

When the planes were all put away for the night the Americans were motored into the city by members of the Rotary club and taken to the King George hotel, where a sumptuous banquet was tendered them by a joint party of city fathers and Rotary club members. His Honor Mayor Young presided as chairman, and at his right sat Captain Street as chief guest of honor. After the banquet the airmen were driven around the city and then taken to the Saskatoon club, where Mayor Young extended to them the official welcome.

The American machines are painted a dark khaki color, with a three-colored circle on the bottom of the under wings and a wolf's head on the side of fuselage. The wing span of the machines is slightly less than the Curtiss plane own by McClelland, but stand higher and are much larger. Each plane is equipped with a 4-B Liberty motor, 12 cylinder, capable of attaining a speed of 150 miles per hour with right wind conditions.

At the airdrome, the aviators were met by Mayor Young and delegations from the city council and the Rotary Club. They were invited to luncheon but had to decline owing to the fact that before leaving them for the night the engines of the planes had to be thoroughly cleaned and oiled.

Captain Street Replies

Replying to Mayor Young at the evening banquet, Captain Street said: "For myself and on behalf of my fellow aviators, I wish to thank you and the people for the splendid reception and treatment that we have had at your hands. I am sure that we of this expedition are very grateful for your hearty welcome. My only regret is that your appreciation of our efforts seems to be a little in advance. So far we have done nothing except

to cover the few miles between here and Mineola safely. I think that this welcome should have been held over until our return trip, when we could have held our heads up and said that we did something. I am sure that with the good wishes tendered to us, our expedition will come through with flying colors and it will be with a great measure of pleasure that I will acquaint my superior officers of the splendid treatment received from you. I can see now why Colonel Hartney, my commanding officer, and brother to Russell Hartney, one of your leading barristers, is such a good officer, coming from the city that he did."

Captain Street mentioned that while in Alaska the expedition expected to do some game hunting, and for the occasion had brought along shotguns and high-powered rifles. "We have been commanded to bring back some Arctic furs," said the Captain, "but the dispatch did not state what we were to wrap them around."

The speaker made mention of one of his flying officers, Lieut. Clifford Nutt. Lieut. Nutt has one of the greatest flying achievements to his credit that has ever been pulled off in the States or in Canada. In command of an expedition, he made a tour of the States for recruits, covering something like 7,000 miles altogether.

"I understand that this expedition will arrive back in the city during the latter part of September." Mayor Young said, when saying good-bye to Captain Street and his companions, "and we shall be very glad to welcome you back to the city."

On behalf of the Vancouver Board of Trade, Major W. S. Weeks, of Vancouver, made a brief speech to Captain Street which was as follows:

Vancouver Interested.

"Your successful arrival in the City of Saskatoon prompts me as a member of the Vancouver Board of Trade to express our good wishes and feelings on your success.

"Without making any great comments upon your world-wide achievement, the Vancouver Board of Trade wishes to express congratulations upon your success on your arrival at your first base in Canada. You are making during your itinerary a visit to many parts of British Columbia which territory is largely dependent upon the City of Vancouver, a city which, for many years, has been commercially associated with the many villages and towns which you will see.

"On behalf of the Vancouver Board of Trade I wish you success and should anything befall you, a telegraph or Marconi which you will find established throughout the North-Western country can readily be found your requirements through this will receive our heartiest attention.

"And, wishing you, gentlemen, the time of your life."

The Great War Veterans band was brought in for the occasion and played "The Star Spangled Banner," "For they are jolly good fellows" and "God Save the King."

The personnel of the expedition is as follows:

Ship 1, Captain St. Clair Street, commander of expedition, pilot, and Sergeant Edmund Henriques, relief pilot and mechanic.

Ship 2, Lieut. Clifford C. Nutt, pilot and Lieut. Eric Nelson, engineering officer and relief pilot.

Ship 3, Lieut. C. Crumrine, pilot

Aerial views of Saskatoon, Saskatchewan. RAA

Hangar at McClelland's Air Field in Saskatoon. RAA

The expedition's Saskatoon hosts pictured with Streett and Kirkpatrick. RAA

With Hardest Part Of Journey To Negotiate U.S. Army Aviators Are Confident Trip Will Be Successful

Captain St. Clair Street Declares That Only Forced Landings Will Mar Good Fortune That Has Accompanied Them—Every Care to Be Taken in Crossing Mountains Which is Most Hazardous of Trip—Leave City Thursday Morning

"No doubt whatsoever is entertained by the American aviators but what the aerial trip to Nome, Alaska, will be made successfully; and to the complete satisfaction of all concerned. We have had a splendid trip so far, and all our anticipations are that this success will follow us. Of course we realise that the hardest part of the journey is still to be negotiated."

Such was the message that Captain St. Clair Street, officer in charge of the American army's aerial expedition from New York to Nome, Alaska, a distance of nine thousand miles, left with The Bulletin when his party reached the Macdonald hotel at eight o'clock Tuesday evening. The entire party of aerial men had worked from two o'clock Tuesday afternoon, in order that everything might be in working condition for the take-off and continuance of the journey westward to be made sometime Thursday morning.

Do Not Anticipate Forced Landings

"Only forced landings will mar the good fortune that has accompanied us, but we do not anticipate any such contingency," was the added comment of Captain Street. He remarked that every care would be taken in crossing the mountainous portion of the tour and expressed the opinion that caution, coupled with the preparation that had been made by the advance officer, Captain Douglas, would leave little in the way to impede a successful completion of the voyage.

Every individual effort is being made by the aviators in order that the anticipated hopes of the United States' war department might be realized. Although pilots and assistants reached the May-Gorman landing grounds about two o'clock Tuesday afternoon, it was not until eight o'clock in the evening that the flying men thought of proceeding to the hotel for their much needed rest. Instead they remained at the aviation grounds taking every possible remedy and precaution so that their planes might be in order for the continuance of the journey Thursday.

Entertained in City

On Thursday evening, the flying visitors were royally entertained by several of Edmonton's public spirited citizens. An informal banquet was held at the Macdonald hotel at which Acting Mayor East, Alderman Charles Hepburn, A. E. Duclos, the Gorman Bros., Captain "Wop" May, John Michaels and a number of local flying men were in attendance. Everything possible is being done to give them a hearty welcome and a good entertainment while in this city.

Taking four hours of actual flying time to come the 300 miles from Saskatoon to Edmonton, American aviators, flying four powerful De Haviland planes, landed at the May-Gorman aerodrome at four minutes after two o'clock Tuesday afternoon. The journey was uneventful except for extra wind power which met the planes on their journey around Manitoba Lake at the boundary line of the two provinces. The landing here completed the seventh phase of the nine thousand mile flight that will take the expedition from Mitchell New York to Nome, Alaska.

"We have had a wonderful trip so
(Continued on Page Three)

The *Morning Bulletin* July 28

AMERICAN AVIATORS ARE DUE TO ARRIVE IN THIS CITY TODAY

Have Reached Portal and Should do 350 Miles in Few Hours

Four American army aeroplanes, under command of Captain St. Claire Street, flying from Mineola, N. Y., to Nome, Alaska, are due to arrive in Saskatoon between the hours of 9 a. m. and 3 p.m. today from North Portal, Sask., a distance of about 350 miles. They will alight at the McClelland and Lobb airdrome north of the city, where they will take aboard 500 gallons of gasoline and a large quantity of oil sufficient to take them from here to Edmonton, which is their next stop. Aviator McClelland expects that if the planes reach Saskatoon in the forenoon, they will take off in the afternoon for Edmonton, but otherwise he anticipates that they will make the city their headquarters for the day.

Great interest has been shown in the flight of these planes, and in anticipation of the large crowd which will wend their way to his flying field Lieut. McClelland has roped off a large portion of the field so that the machines will not be tampered with.

Official reasons given for the flight are the establishment of a direct air route from the United States to Asia, and the photographing of unmapped and inaccessible areas of Alaska.

The itinery and constructive distance in miles to be travelled are: Michel Field to Erie, Pa., 350 miles; Grand Rapids, 350 miles; Fargo, 350 miles; Saskatoon, 350 miles; Edmonton 300 miles; Jasper, 300; Prince George, 300; Hazelton, 250; Wrangel, Alaska, 210; White Horse, Yukon, 300; Dawson, 350; Fairbanks, 250; Ruby, 250, and Nome, 300.

Saskatoon Phoenix July 26

Edmonton Journal

EDMONTON, ALBERTA, TUESDAY, JULY 27, 1920   SIXTEEN PAGES

DAILY CIRCULATION
JULY
17,226

GHT AIRS MARKS FINAL OF CUP CONTESTS

Alaska Flyers Make Fast Trip From Saskatoon

SS ARE D ON RRIVAL

Sends
chalf of
ion

ONEY;
K; ARE
GUESTS

sponds to
ayor of
n

—A hundred
ited the over-
mperial Press
foot in Can-
morning for a
nada. Premier
f the federal
eutenant-gov-
presidents of
Sir Arthur
in, President
nd scores of
out the do-
y welcome to
asing appre-
to Imperial
tal Press con-

ame
premier of
rovernment of

the dele-
ress confer-
nvite you to
stitution of
d conditions
me at your
d I assure
and a warm
the purpose
the people
information
f this coun-
you, people
parts of the
he of great

ed Them
Minister of jus-
tion, P. U
cabinet; Sir
A. A. Tas-
n, of Quebec
Hon. W., L.
V; Hon. Chas.
shard; John
n, Manitoba
a, Alberta,
good wishes
sference,
from the
9 a.m. and
udomouto on
ax attendance
dny, Sydney
ignalized the
the town, the
rman of the
the mayor's

that we are
are over-
and whole-
le Canada
of treating
gave the
of the over-
perial Press
S. Victorian
ray harbor at
s continues;
of the city
there has
flood of
da, and
nada a

Flying From New York to Nome

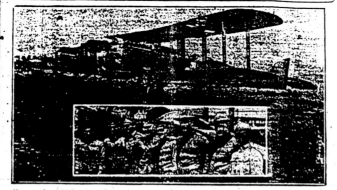

Here are the eight American airmen who are making the longest flight ever attempted on this continent—from New York to Nome, Alaska. The upper picture shows a line-up of three machines and the lower shows the crews. A great part of the flight is over Canadian territory.

POLISH SUPPLY TRAIN STRIPPED BY GERMANS WHILE IN TRANSIT FROM OCCUPIED ZONE ON RHINE

This Action In Contempt of Allies Took Place at Marburg—Lloyd-George and Millerand to Discuss Russian Situation at Boulogne

COBLENZ, July 27.—(Associated Press)—A Polish supply train of thirteen cars bearing arms and ammunition from France, with five Polish and one French officer on board, which left the area occupied by United States troops Saturday evening, was held up by German police and a crowd of civilians at Marburg, 60 miles east of Coblenz, Sunday afternoon.

The Germans completely stripped the cars of their war material and the train crews refused to convey them further.

No Treaty For Some Days

LONDON, July 27.—News as to the signing of an armistice between Poland and the Soviet government of Russia is not expected for some days, the Soviet commissioner for foreign affairs, Tchitcherin, having signalized the conference in London at which all the Baltic states are to be represented.

Mr. Lloyd-George and M. Millerand have arranged to meet and consider the preliminaries.

To Hold Conference

PARIS, July 27.—Premier Millerand, accompanied by Marshal Foch, Frederic Francois-Marsal, minister of finance, and Philippe Berthelot, political director of the foreign office, left at eight o'clock Tuesday morning for Boulogne, where he will discuss with Premier Lloyd George the Russian soviet proposal for a conference between the allies and representatives of the Russian soviet government.

It is reported that Premier Millerand, wounded by the British government on this question, gave as preliminary condition to entering negotiations with the Russians, the acknowledgment by the soviet of international engagements of former Russian governments and confirmation by the Russian people of the soviet's authority.

The probability is also expressed that M. Millerand will refuse to agree to the request in the Russian note for the surrender of General Wrangel, the anti-Bolshevist leader in southern Russia, and that he will ask the United States to participate in the London conference if it be held.

All the newspapers attach considerable importance to the new situation resulting from the proposal of M. Tchitcherin, and Tuesday's meeting of the British and French premiers.

With the exception of the Socialist organs, the newspapers are unanimous in support of the government's plan to demand of the soviet government recognition of former Russian governments.

According to the Echo de Paris, M. Millerand will ask that the government of General Wrangel and other governments in support of what formerly were parts of Russia, be represented at the proposed London conference.

Denies Suggestion

BERLIN, July 27.—The suggestion that Germany had been tempted to join forces with soviet Russia in order to regain her old bla.

CABINET STILL MUCH AGAINST MARTIAL LAW

Report Will Not Take This Step to Control Ireland

PERLEY TO SIGN TURKISH TREATY FOR DOMINION

Leaves London For Paris as Canada's Official Representative

TURKISH DELEGATES LATE IN ARRIVING

Fall of Adrianople Accomplished Only After Very Heavy Fighting

(Special Staff Correspondence of Edmonton Journal, Copyright Cross-Atlantic Newspaper Service)

LONDON, July 27.—Sir George Perley is leaving for Paris today to sign the Turkish and Schleswig treaties on behalf of the Dominion of Canada.

Will Not Sign Today

LONDON, July 27.—(Associated Press).—The Turkish delegates will not sign the peace treaty Tuesday, owing to their inability to reach Paris in time. A rather apologetic note from the Constantinople government, to the British foreign office, Monday, said that traffic interruptions, which probably were the result of military operations, prevented the delegates arriving in the time given by the allies, which expires Tuesday night.

Severe Losses Are Reported on Each Side

(Special Staff Correspondence of Edmonton Journal, Copyright Cross-Atlantic Newspaper Service)

LONDON, July 27.—Adrianople is reported occupied by the Greeks, after heavy fighting, with severe losses on both sides. Parts of the city were set on fire by Turkish rebels, who are said to be heading for Kirklisse.

After signing the treaty, the Turkish government will be given two months in which to restore order in Asia Minor, it is learned by mail. During this period.

DEPUTY MAYOR EAST GREETS AMERICAN AIRMEN FROM AEROPLANE OVER HIGHLANDS

Flyers Land By Mistake on Portage Avenue Grounds But Immediately Proceed to May-Gorman Field; Make Good Time on the Trip From Saskatoon to Edmonton

Four De Haviland 4-B biplanes, manned by members of the Alaska Flying expedition, made a successful flight on the Saskatoon-Edmonton leg of their transcontinental trip, arriving in the centre of the city at 2:12 p.m. The U.S. army fliers left Saskatoon at 9:51, making the estimated distance of 300 miles at the rate of four miles in three minutes. Capt. Wop May, with Acting-Mayor James East as passenger, flew out to the city's outskirts over the Highlands to meet the visitors, and escorted them the last few miles.

Arrangements were originally made to have the Alaskan party land at the May-Gorman aerodrome where supplies of oil and gasoline had been placed in readiness, but while flying over Portage avenue the visitors sighted the Edmonton Aeroplane's landing place and descended. Consequently there was a delay of some twenty minutes before the error was rectified, and the original plans adhered to. For miles on either side of the St. Albert trail automobiles were parked, and the visitors were enthusiastically received.

The reasons for the flight to Nome were twofold. One is to establish an aerial route to the northwest corner of the American continent, so that should military considerations require it, it would be possible to move the U.S. army air units to the continent of Asia by direct flight. The second reason for the long journey is for the purpose of photographing inaccessible areas in Alaska which have never been mapped.

The expedition is commanded by Capt. St. Claire Street, who carries Sergt. Edmond Henriques, an observer and mechanician. Plane No. 3 is piloted by Lieut. C. H. Crumrine, photographic officer of the party. The second in command is Lieut. Clifford C. Nutt, who is accompanied by Lieut. Eric H. Nelson, also a pilot and engineering officer of the flight. The fourth plane is piloted by Lieut. Ross Kirkpatrick with Master Electrician Joseph E. English as observer and mechanicien.

VOICES CARRIED 2,000 MILES BY WIRELESS PHONE

Sir Stuart Campbell Hears Call For Daily Mail Reporter

ONE ON ATLANTIC, OTHER IN LON ON

Victorian's Passengers Talk to Newspaper Men In Newfoundland

(Special Staff Correspondence of Edmonton Journal, Copyright Cross-Atlantic Newspaper Service)

LONDON, July 27.—Sir Stuart Campbell, editor of the Daily Mail, talked to his office here today by telephone, although he was in mid-Atlantic on the Victorian. Sir Stuart is a delegate to the Imperial Press conference of Ottawa and is en route to Montreal.

'FROM SEA TO SEA' CANADA DEVICE ON NEW COAT OF ARMS

Design Has Been Forwarded to College of Heralds, London

OTTAWA, July 27.—The design for the new Canadian coat-of-arms has gone to the College of Heralds. The procedure is somewhat involved. After approval by the Canadian government, the design goes to the College of Heralds, where, it is possible, some minor technical changes may be suggested. Subsequently, formal approval is given by the king-in-council on instructions issued to the Earl Marshal, who is head of the college.

The new coat-of-arms bears the device, "A Mari Usque Ad Mare" (from sea to sea). It is taken from the singularly appropriate line in the seventy-second psalm, "He shall have dominion also from sea to sea."

Approval of the coat-of-arms was the last act of the Borden government.

ANNOUNCEMENT

WAGE INCREASE

VANCOUVER ISLAND

 *To Edmonton*

Another early morning takeoff was scheduled from Saskatoon for the 300-mile trip to Edmonton. The planes did not get away until almost 10 a.m., and the crew had to shake every hand in the crowd gathered for the takeoff.

Twenty minutes from the city brought the planes over the lake district, a large undeveloped area that would prove to be difficult to land on due to the swampy terrain. They were flying into a 20-m.p.h. headwind and tried every elevation from 100 feet up to 7,000 feet. But the wind seemed the same at all levels. These conditions are peculiar to flat, prairie country.

They flew over Lake Manitou and followed the Battle River valley for 50 miles, leaving it when Beaver Hills Lake was sighted. Close to Edmonton, they saw their first pine and spruce forests.

Circling the city to take photographs, Streett spotted a landing field in the northeast section of the city. Capt. "Wop" May and his passenger, Acting Mayor James East took off to escort the planes to his airfield. When the four planes landed, with May right behind, they found that they had landed at Jock McNeill's air harbor not the May-Gorman aerodrome. All their supplies and a large crowd were waiting at the aerodrome, so the crews took off again and 20 minutes later made the correct landing.

Nutt had broken a wing skid and bent his right aileron horn on landing, and Streett's gas tank had sprung a leak. It was decided to stay in Edmonton until a thorough overhauling of the planes was completed. The next leg of the journey, flying over the Rocky Mountains, would be the most challenging, so every precaution had to be taken to ensure the safety of the planes and crew.

As Captain Streett wrote in his journal that night, "From now on it would be necessary to move with the greatest caution."

The crewmen were honored at a banquet that night at the Macdonald Hotel.

Frank Oliver, publisher of the *Edmonton Bulletin* made the following comments:

" Here it is only 44 years since I journeyed for two months to arrive in Edmonton by ox-cart. It's only 11 years since I saw Blériot first flying the English Channel. Now you gentlemen are en route to faraway Alaska. This expedition is as much of a contrast to that feat of 11 years ago as were the ox-carts of the past with modern means of transportation."

American Flyers Reach Edmonton in 4 Hours 12 Minutes

LARGE CROWD GATHERED AT AERODROME AND GAVE
THREE CHEERS AS PLANES TOOK THE AIR—
MET AT EDMONTON BY THE ACTING
MAYOR IN PLANE

EDMONTON, July 27.—(Canadian Press.)—The Alaska flying expedition aeroplanes of the American Army Service arrived here at 2.12 p.m., and were met by Acting Mayor James East and Alderman Charles Hepburn, chairman of the civic reception committee, in aeroplanes piloted by Captain May and Lieut. Gorman.

With cheers from hundreds of throats ringing in their ears above the roaring hum of their motors, the United States army flyers in their four De-Haviland 4-B planes, who reached Saskatoon from Mineola, N.Y., Monday afternoon, took off from McClelland's aerodrome shortly before 10 o'clock this morning on the next jump in their trip to Nome, Alaska.

A large crowd collected early at the flying field and the four powerful machines, glittering in the bright sun, were the centre of attraction. The first plane took the air at 9.51, and was followed in quick succession by its three companions, the last leaving the ground at 9.59.

Lieut. H. S. McClelland and the Keng Wah Aviation School machine, piloted by Lieut. McNeil, were also in the air and the sight of the six big birds swooping, zooming and circling over the aerodrome provided the spectators with a genuine thrill.

"THREE CHEERS"

As the first unit of the Alaska flying expedition taxied across the field, Mayor A. MacG. Young lifted his hat and called for three cheers. The response was instant and unanimous and the land-lubbers tacked on a "tiger" for good measure.

The American airmen fly from Saskatoon to Edmonton, a distance of 300 miles. From Edmonton they jump to Jasper, Alta., 200 miles, and then 200 miles across the Rockies to Prince George, B.C. From that point the course follows the coast line to the Yukon and the final destination.

AIRPLANE MAIL

Included in Capt. Street's luggage when he took off this morning was an envelope containing a copy of The Star, addressed to the editor of the Nugget, which is the evening news-paper in Nome, Alaska, the airmen's destination.

"This has been the most wonderful reception since we left New York," Capt. St. Clair Street, commander of the expedition, said when he shook hands with Mayor Young. "On our way back we may arrange a longer stop in Saskatoon. This is a great little city and you have a great bunch of citizens. God bless you all."

As each airplane left the ground it circled higher and higher until all four were in "diamond" formation. Then, after a final swing over the crowd and a last hand-wave, they struck out into the west, travelling at a fast clip until they were but specks in the sky.

McCLELAND TO IMPERIAL

Meantime Lieut. H. S McClelland headed his plane south for Imperial, Sask., where he is due to fly today in a sports day program, while the aviator of the Chinese plane did a little reckless stunting, swooping low over the crowd and spoiling the effect of scores of heartily eaten breakfasts.

There was a light wind out of the west, but the sky was practically cloudless, and the Americans estimated they would make the Alberta capital in record time.

Officials of the U.S. Air Service at Washington appointed N. C. Byers, of Saskatoon, official timekeeper. Mr. Byers wired Washington when the machines arrived and also when they left today. He also sent the official time to the mayor of Edmonton.

Throughout the afternoon and night the planes were guarded by a member of the city police force, detailed by Chief G. M. Donald. Captain Street was grateful for this effort at co-operation and said he greatly appreciated the kind forethought of the police chief.

Saskatoon Daily Star July 27

Portion of May-Gorman Field at Edmonton, Alberta. RAA

The four planes on May-Gorman Field. The crowds were typical of every stop along the way as many people had never seen an airplane up close. SI

The four planes lined up on May-Gorman Field without the crowds. PAA #72.154/15A

Guards shown in front of one of the planes at Edmonton. PAA #72.154/18

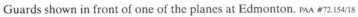

Owing to the interrupted cable service the Sentinel is unable to give much news today concerning airplanes of the transcontinental flight. It is evident that after the mishaps that attended the early part of the flight the squadron gave up all thought of making a speed record. As the flyers have been making only one leg a day for the past week it is presumed that plan will be continued for the remainder of the flight, and that we cannot expect the squadron here before some time next week

The blowing of the mill whistle and the ringing of the various bells will proclaim in advance the coming of the planes to Wrangell. The Barrington people will be prepared to provide transportation for all who do not go to the landing field in their own boats.

As the flight from Hazelton to Wrangell will be a most difficult one it is expected that the flyers will stop over night in Wrangell before proceeding to Whitehorse.

EDMONTON—(Tuesday)—The four army planes enroute from New York to Nome arrived here at 2:12 this afternoon from Saskatoon, making the 300 mile flight in record time.

Capt. St. Clair Streett, squadron commander, plans to resume the flight Thursday morning. The next leg will carry the planes to Jasper, 200 miles from here.

SASKATOON, Sask. (Monday) The four Alaska-bound planes arrived here today.

Capt. St. Clair Streett, commander of the squadron, announced here today, that their total flying time from Minneola, N.Y. to Saskatoon is less than fifteen hours, although they have been more than a week en route.

PORTAL, North Dakota—The planes arrived here from Fargo making the 290-mile flight in three hours and ten minutes.

A type of plane quite different from those used by the American flyers in the World war are employed in making the flight from New York to Nome. For this flight the Army is using the new DeHaviland 4-B, which should not be confused with the old DeHaviland 4 of the War service.

Many important changes distinguish the new 4-B plane from its predecessor. In the old type the pilot, seated just in rear of the motor and in front of the gasoline tank, had practically no chance at all to escape being crushed between the two in the event of a crash.

The pilot using the new plane in the Alaskan flight is seated behind the gasoline tank, which in turn is right behind the motor. This arrangement, according to the construction experts, greatly improves the flyer's chances, practically removing the danger of death from an ordinary crash.

Another advantage is claimed for the plane which is having its searching tryout on the long trip to Alaska is that the passenger's seat is immediately behind the pilot, allowing easy communication between the two men. This, it is said, should prove extremely valuable on the laps of the trip which lies over uncharted territory.

In recent tryouts between New York and Washington, a certain pilot while flying in a fog failed to notice a three-crested ridge for which he was headed. The passenger, however, being where he could see, sensed the danger and called the pilot's attention to it. He immediately caused the plane to rise, just in time to miss the trees.

The Liberty motors used in the Alaskan flight will be equipped with an intake manifold stack.

In order to minimize the danger from fire, in case of a backfire from any of the cylinders which might ignite the gasoline in the carburetor, the intake stack affords an outlet over the top of the engine for the flame and prevents loose gasoline deposited on the engine from catching fire.

In a statement on the Alaskan flight issued recently, the War Department says:

"The Army has taken every precaution and has sought in every way to reduce the risks to the flyers. The obstacles of nature which must be overcome, especially after leaving Jasper, Alberta, are sufficient to try the stoutest heart. On this leg the Canadian rockies are encountered, and this is one of the most rugged and inaccessible regions in the Northwest."

The Juneau Empire says:

Maybe when the New York-to-Nome flyers reach Alaska they can make better time. There'll not be so many towns to stop at, and once those Yukon and Tanana valley mosquitoes get after them, they won't tarry long at any one place.

The Douglas Island News says:

Those army planes that are said to be on the way north from New York are not making any speed records. If they don't get here pretty soon Alaskans will be saying, "There ain't no such animal."

The Wrangell Sentinel
July 15

LEAKY GAS TANK CAUSES POSTPONEMENT AIR FLIGHT TO JASPER UNTIL FRIDAY

Every Precaution Being Taken to Guard Against Mishaps on Hazardous Journey Through Mountains; Landing Places Are Few and Far Between

Another day's delay in the New York to Nome, Alaska, flight being made by the four American army aeroplanes, has been caused by a leak in the gas tank of one of the machines, and some minor defects which were discovered in the overhauling given the planes Wednesday. Consequently the hop-off which was scheduled for this morning has been postponed until 9 o'clock Friday.

Capt. Street and his mechanic realize that the most difficult part of their hazardous journey lies immediately ahead of them. On the jump from Edmonton to Jasper they enter the Rocky mountains about sixty miles, and from Jasper to Prince George a landing place in case of trouble would be practically impossible to find, as here the mountain ranges are highest and all heavily wooded. There are very few clearings in the district, and with this in view every possible form of trouble must be guarded against.

The aviators plan to cross the mountains at a height of 2,000 feet above the highest peaks to avoid the dangerous wind pockets that are known to exist in mountain flying; a fact that was amply proven in the negotiation last year of the Kicking Horse pass from Vancouver to Calgary.

Edmonton Journal
July 29

To Jasper

Before leaving Edmonton, information was obtained from the old settlers of the areas as to terrain, climate, landmarks, height of the mountains and the character of the landing fields in Jasper. This would be one of the most dangerous legs of the trip, even though it was only 197 miles away.

Heavy clothing, blankets and additional food was loaded aboard the planes in case of a force-down in the cold, snowy mountains. The additional weight in the planes caused some problems on takeoff.

After four days of work on the planes, the expedition was ready to take off on the morning of July 31. The weather was misty, and a course was set to follow the Pembina River for many miles. The pilots soon discovered that on reaching altitude, the clouds hung too low for them to see the river and completely hid the mountain range over which the planes would have to pass. Reluctantly, Streett signaled the planes to return to Edmonton.

This was the first time since leaving New York that all four planes had to return at the same time.

When he landed back at Edmonton, Streett communicated with Jasper and found out the weather was clear there, but halfway there, at Edson, fog and low clouds were reported, so they decided to wait until the next morning.

At 9:37 a.m. on Aug. 1, the four planes again left Edmonton with bright and clear skies. As they flew again over the Pembina River country the pilots saw the very rough terrain, with rivers flowing through deep gorges and thick forests. The entire country had been devastated by forest fires. Millions of jackpines and fir trees had been burned. A crash landing there could only be fatal.

Reaching Rocky River, the pilots noticed the foothills giving way to the high and rugged Rocky Mountain peaks. The snow-clad mountain tops, shining almost pink in the sunlight, burst suddenly into view.

Turning north they picked up the Athabaska River, passed over the little town of Pocahontas, flew between Jasper Lake and Brides Lake, and swung into the valley of the Athabaska. They were flying at 6,000 feet over some of the most beautiful and rugged country in North America. As Streett mentioned in his *National Geographic* article:

"Our motors hummed sturdily over this terrible landscape—terrible to the anxious pilot who is constantly straining his eyes to select the site for a forced landing should his motor fail."

SECOND EFFORT TO REACH JASPER IS SUCCESSFUL

U. S. Flying Expedition Forced to Turn Back on Saturday; Dense Clouds

STREET'S ORDERS TO TAKE HIS TIME

First Landing Safely Accomplished In Mountains; Next Leg to Prince George

After two hours and twenty minutes actual flying time the American-New York to Nome expedition landed at Jasper Sunday at 11 a.m., mountain time, according to a dispatch received by The Journal from Capt. S. Claire Street, who is in command of the four planes. The journey was made entirely without incident, being the second attempt made to enter the Rockies through the Yellowhead Pass.

On Saturday the planes were forced to turn back after traveling sixty-nine miles, when they encountered dense, low hanging clouds, making it impossible for them to continue, so they turned back to Edmonton to await more favorable conditions. Capt. Street explained that his orders were to take his time and get through successfully, and this he is doing; no attempt at setting a speed record or anything like that is being made.

The landing at Jasper, says a wire from The Journal's correspondent there was made in the following order: Plane No. 4, 11 a.m.; No. 3, 11:02; No. 2, 11:05 and No. 1, 11:07. The expedition planned to get away on the next leg of the journey, from Jasper to Prince George some time this morning if conditions were suitable. On this part of the trip they will cross the highest peaks in the Rockies, and will require clear skies for the purpose.

Edmonton Journal,
August 2

As they flew along the river at 1,000 feet among the high mountains and deep gorges, a flat plain covered with jackpine and quaking aspen came into view. At the mouth of the valley the Snaring River empties into the Athabaska River from the west. Beside the Snaring River lay the landing field at Jasper.

Camp at Jasper Park. Notice the American flag on the right side of the photo. RAA

After three hours in the air, the planes landed without incident on a very smooth runway. It was prepared under the supervision of Col. Maynard Rogers, superintendent of Jasper National Park. It was hoped that this field would eventually be the headquarters for a squadron of fire-spotting airplanes.

Most of the residents of this remote country had never seen an airplane, and they gathered around the machines asking many questions. Col. Rogers had provided a Chinese cook, supplies and several tents with pine-bough bedding. The crewmen enjoyed swimming and fishing, but the mosquitoes eventually were biting more than the fish. It got so cold that night that the men had to roll up in their blankets close to the camp fires.

Crews going over the planes prior to takeoff from Jasper Park landing field. UAA

Mount Robson. RAA

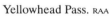

Yellowhead Pass. RAA

Grand Trunk Pacific Railroad Bridge at Jasper Park. The landing field was just below the bridge. RAA

Aerial view of the town of Jasper, Alberta. RAA

# To Prince George and Hazelton

The flights through British Columbia, both northward and return, proved to be the most eventful and time-consuming on the mission. Northbound, there was an 11-day layover in Prince George for repairs, and southbound, a 20-day layover for repairs and weather clearance at the Diamond C Ranch near Glenora, B.C. Less than first class landing sites and poor weather in the province proved to be the undoing of the flight plans.

After an overnight stint at Jasper, Alberta, the fliers were ready to tackle the Yellowhead Pass through the Rockies. This would be the first traverse of the Yellowhead, and indeed of the province, by an aircraft at this latitude. The photographs taken by the flight photographer and the description of the flight through the mountains tend to dramatize the journey. The Yellowhead is the easiest pass through the Rockies, and the Grand Trunk Pacific rail line provided an easy road map to follow. All went well except that Captain Streett suffered an oil problem with his aircraft and had to return to Jasper for adjustments soon after takeoff. The oil flowing from an overfilled tank caught on fire when it hit the hot exhaust stack. Henriques, who was flying at the time, side-slipped the plane, hoping to land in the water. But the fire extinguished itself when the plane tipped in the other direction. The other three fliers continued on to Prince George, arriving in the early afternoon of Aug. 2, 1920.

There was an interesting set of arrangements and rules to be observed for the arrival of the expedition in Prince George. Presumably these were established in part at least by the advanced planning party of Captain Douglas and Captain LeRoyer. Local parties had also established an information system for monitoring the progress of the flight. The Grand Trunk Pacific agent at McBride, B.C., would signal the Prince George office when the aircraft passed over his office. The roundhouse whistle at Prince George would then be blown several times to advise the community of the approaching aircraft.

The landing strip was laid out on what is now known as Central Avenue in Prince George. An area 100 yards wide by 300 yards long was identified with corner markings, a smoke pot and a large "T" on the ground to indicate the direction to be used in approaching the field. The general public, motor cars, dogs and other animals were to be kept clear of the area. After landing, the aircraft were not to be handled, and smoking around the machines was prohibited.

The engine trouble at Jasper separated Captain Streett from the other three aircraft by about three hours, and by the time he reached Prince George he encountered a severe thunderstorm. At first he overshot Prince George due to the heavy rain and poor visibility, but on turning back he was able to see houses and a road. After searching the community, he was able to locate the designated landing field. In Captain Streett's words:

"Finally a blaze of light on the ground to my right indicated that a flare had been lighted to guide me. Flying low I observed the three airplanes of my flight huddled together in a blinding rain, while around them was grouped a number of motor cars. I made a blind landing. As luck would have it, I hit the edge of the field and smashed my left wing and tore away the whole side of the stabilizer. Ten feet more to my right would have given me an open path."

The other aircraft had arrived without injury with the exception of Lieutenant Crumrine's No. 3 aircraft, which blew a tire and hit a small obstruction at the end of the field. This set the aircraft on its nose, damaging the propeller and marring the wing. Captain Streett's aircraft required the services of a local cabinet-maker, Mr. Charles Sinclair, to repair some wood struts and spars on the damaged wings. A local tailor was engaged to repair the torn linen fabric on the damaged sections.

The second in command of the mission, Lt. Clifford C. Nutt, also provided insight into the Prince George stopover when he wrote in the *Air Service News Letter* immediately following the return to New York:

"We got into Prince George just ahead of a rain storm and without Captain Streett, but a wire from him explained his mishap at Jasper. We lighted flares to aid him in finding the field. The outline of the field was of course indefinite, so when Street [sic] came in he had good speed and overshot, rolling out of the field itself into a cut-over stretch beyond, where he struck a stump that took off about four feet of the left wing, breaking both main spars and tearing all the ribs out, also the left half of his horizontal stabilizer and the aileron. So, we got busy

on the job with the help of a big Swede carpenter who was a wonder and who had some excellent spruce timber. He framed up the wing for us, built ribs and spars for the stabilizer and ailerons. Each one of us had a piece of linen for patching so we pooled our supply and covered the wing. Lieutenant Kirkpatrick, the only chemist we had in the party, mixed up the dope for the fabric but it proved not very efficient as the linen was about as flabby when it dried as it had been before wetting. But we took a chance on the new wing anyhow. For almost ten days in all, we got our first acquaintance of a frontier town. We got acquainted with hard-boiled miners of the old type, with lumberjacks, great tall Scotchmen and little French Canadians, who came in about twice a week just for the fun of spending their money. One old fellow, Scotty by name, was about

seven feet tall and weighed about three hundred pounds, they said, when he was sober. He looked as if he weighed a good deal more drunk, which was all the time apparently."

The Prince George interlude had consumed 11 days, from Aug. 2 to Aug. 12. Consequently, this elapsed time allowed much contact with the community. The photographs taken by local trades people and dignitaries produced a memorable record in the total story of the expedition. At the Aug. 3 meeting of the Prince George Board of Trade a decision was made to host a banquet and dance in honor of the visitors who would be guests of the Board. The function was held in the Ritts-Kifer Hall on Thursday, Aug. 5, and was well-attended.

Touching up the village "vamp" at Prince George. RAA

One of the "belles" at Prince George. RAA

Nutt's plane, the *Kittie IV* seemed to attract the women. Here a group is standing beside his aircraft in Prince George. TMC

Getting ready to repair Streett's plane at Prince George with Kirkpatrick's plane in the background. TMC

Streett's Plane No. 1 after repairs had been completed. Barrels were used to prop up the aircraft during repairs. TMC, FRANK HEWLETT COLL.

Kirkpatrick's Plane No. 4 at Prince George getting spruced up. Notice the propped open storage area hood at the rear of the fuselage. TMC

Nutt's Plane No. 2 (top) and Kirkpatrick's Plane No. 4 (bottom) ready to take off from Prince George. TMC

Hazelton, B.C.

An advanced party consisting of Captain Douglas from Washington and Captain LeRoyer from Ottawa made an inspection of possible Hazelton landing sites in June 1920. They selected an area close to the hospital in Hazelton.

While the Prince George repair program was underway in August, Captain Streett and Lieutenant Nutt travelled to Hazelton on the train to review the proposed landing site. They were unsatisfied with the initial suggestion and scouted the vicinity for better prospects. They eventually decided on a good, broad and lengthy strip of land close to the bank of the Bulkley River, right where it joins the Skeena River, at

a location called Mission Point. The only problem was that the field was covered with an oat crop owned by George Biernes. An arrangement was made to clear a section of the oat field and have it compacted for aircraft landing.

The matter of landing field dimensions caused concern with several sites. Apparently, the advanced party responsible for selecting suitable landing strips underestimated the requirements for length and for rise clearances after takeoff. Lieutenant Nutt relates the necessity for relocating the landing site at Hazelton and problems with the rather restricted facility at Prince George. The DH-4 aircraft had no brakes, and if the landing speed was more than anticipated, soon the pilot would run out of desirable real estate.

Repairs at Prince George were finally completed on Aug. 12, and the flight prepared to leave the following day. At 9:05 a.m. on Friday the 13th, they departed for Hazelton. It was a lucky Friday the 13th. The weather was fine, and they easily followed the rail line west, passing over the communities of Burns Lake and Smithers and arriving at Hazelton in slightly over three hours. The pre-arranged landing strip in the Biernes oat field proved adequate, and all fliers enjoyed good landings with no mishaps. Although Biernes had rolled the field, the ground was too loose for takeoff, and an assembled army of sightseers, including many native people, was recruited to march up and down on the field to pack it even firmer for takeoff.

The flight stayed overnight at Hazelton, and the visitors were treated to dining, dancing and revelry. On the evening of arrival, the local War Veterans hosted a dinner and dance in honor of the fliers. Welcome speeches were made, a toast to King George V was offered and an appreciation speech was given by Capt. St. Clair Streett. The fliers were duly impressed by the large number of people attending the reception. Dancing continued to the wee hours of the morning after midnight refreshments and one o'clock ices.

A favorable weather report was received from Wrangell, and on the following day, Saturday, Aug. 14, the flight departed from Hazelton at 2:30 p.m. The Hazelton stop was one of the more accommodating since leaving New York.

The four planes lined up on the oat field landing strip at Hazelton. This is at Mission Point where the Bulkley River joins the Skeena at South Hazelton. View looking south with the river just behind the photographer. TMC

The same scene as above, taken in 1997 by Trelle Morrow. The planes were parked just to the right of the two telephone poles. The 1920 photo shows the poles on the left. They were taken down and an underground line was installed when Mission Point was used as an airstrip. Later, the poles were set on the right hand side of the road. TMC

The Parent family, mother and three boys, in front of Nutt's plane at Hazelton. TMC, PARENT COLL.

The Parent twins, Delcourt and Louis with brother, Douglas, and two British Columbia Police officers at Hazelton. TMC, PARENT COLL.

The Parent family, along with many other residents of Hazelton, viewing the planes. The two small boys in the foreground are twins, Delcourt and Louis Parent. They still live in Hazelton. TMC, PARENT COLL.

Top: Captain Streett at Hazelton with the Parent twins in the front seat and their brother in the rear. Left: Photo taken later in the day of Captain Streett with Sergeant Henriques in the background. TMC, PARENT COLL.

British Columbia Provincial Police guards at Hazelton. RAA

Taking on gas at Hazelton with Rocher Deboule Mountain in the background. RAA

Plane No. 2 taking off from the oat field at Hazelton. View looking southwest. BULKLEY VALLEY MUSEUM, SMITHERS, B.C.

EW YORK TO NOME AIRFLIGHT. HAZELTON B.C AUG 14 1920

To Wrangell

At 1:30 p.m. on Aug. 14, all the planes left Hazelton, although with great difficulty. They got up to 6,000 feet but soon had to climb up to 10,000 feet to cross over the rugged mountains and glaciers below. The sun shone down strongly on the fliers, and the glare nearly blinded them.

It was hard to appreciate the beautiful scenery below because they had to concentrate on the hum of their engines. With no place to make a forced landing, there was no room for error or engine trouble.

This went on nearly two hours before they recognized the Nash River, partly from their maps, which proved to be very inaccurate, and partly from the descriptions given them at their last stop. Then came the Stewart Arm, and they knew they had Alaska in sight.

Just south of Stewart they dropped down to 5,000 feet, crossed over Behm Canal, then 10 minutes later over Bradford Canal. Then Wrangell was sighted. A smudge pot marked the landing field.

The field on Sergief Island appeared to be excellent from the air. Kirkpatrick was the first to set down, and the others soon followed. What they found was a landing field in a bed of salt marsh grass immersed in over a foot of water in places. Landing in water was more disconcerting than dangerous, and the airmen were throughly drenched. They later found out that Wrangell was at that moment experiencing the highest tide of the summer: 19 feet. No one at Wrangell had thought about this problem beforehand. Richard Suratt, representing the Fox News Agency, took movies of the landing, perhaps the first aviation movies taken in Alaska. To stop on the soggy field, Nelson and Long climbed out of their seats upon landing and rode on the tails of their planes to slow them down. The mayor of Wrangell, J.G. Grant, met the planes and J.W. Pritchett, editor of *The Wrangell Sentinel*, was handed a copy of the *New York Times*.

The town of Wrangell was seven miles from Sergief Island, so crew and the people who had come to meet them were hauled over by boat. Another banquet was held in the fliers' honor. At the close of the dinner, Mayor Grant requested J.W. Pritchett to read two cablegrams:

(From the Governor)

Grant, Mayor
Wrangell
Had hoped to get to Wrangell to greet Army Aviators, but find I am unable to leave. Express my welcome and the welcome of the Territory to Captain Streett and his daring companions, and wish them every success in their trip to Nome.

RIGGS (Thomas)
Governor

(From the Mayor of Juneau)

J. G. Grant, Mayor
Wrangell
Please extend on behalf of the citizens of the Capital City of Alaska a hearty greeting to the gallant aviators who are making their entry into Alaska through your city and a cordial invitation to fly over our city and Gastineau channel where six thousand Alaskans are eager to see their flight.

R. E. Robertson
Mayor

Radio station at Wrangell. RAA

THE WRANGELL SENTINEL

VOL. XIX. NO. 34 | WRANGELL, ALASKA, THURSDAY, AUGUST 19, 1920 | PRICE TEN CENTS

First Planes From States Arrive in Alaska Saturday

Aerial Trail Blazers to the Far North Fly From Hazelton to Wrangell in Two Hours and Twenty-seven Minutes.

Saturday, August 14, 1920, Will Go Down in History as One of the Great Moments in History of the Northland

Capt. St. Clair Streett and His Daring Companions, Undaunted by Previous Difficulties, Arrive in Fine Spirits, and Receive Enthusiastic Welcome

The arrival on Alaskan soil near Wrangell of four army airplanes from New York at 4:08 Saturday afternoon was a history making event, the significance and importance of which will be more fully realized and appreciated in future years than at present.

The Mayor Declares a Holiday

When it became known that the airplane squadron was expected to arrive Saturday afternoon Mayor Grant declared a holiday. Flags were hoisted over the principal buildings of the town. Early in the forenoon the blowing of the mill whistle and the ringing of bells gave the signal that it was time to put out the cat and start for the landing field. The town of Wrangell was soon deserted of its population. All during the forenoon small boats were leaving for the landing field on Sergeif island. At noon the Barrington Transportation company's Hazel B No. 3, which is so popular with Wrangell people left the City float having in tow a big scow and both boat and scow loaded to the limit with passengers.

No one seemed to expect the planes to arrive before 2:30 p. m., but after that time there was much watching, and several times distant specks of cloud caused excitement for a minute or so and then disappeared. No message had been received at Wrangell stating that the flyers had actually left Hazelton, and at 4 o'clock people were beginning to get restless and say they did not think the planes were coming that day.

Planes Are Sighted

Just as one family were getting ready to go back to their gasboat someone shouted, "There they come!" at the same time pointing in the direction of Wrangell. No one had any difficulty in seeing the approaching planes and all was excitement. Sergeant W. W. McLaughlin hastily lit a smudge and by that time the buzzing of the machines in the air could be heard.

Plane No. 4 the First to Land

The planes circled around over the island several times making an observation of the landing field. Lieutenant Ross Kirkpatrick of Plane No. 4 gave the spectators a real thrill when he made a pass by the crowd only a short distance in the air going 60 miles an hour. He then made a wide circle slowing down as he went, and upon again reaching the field he first touched ground only a few feet in front of the crowd. The machine stopped very shortly after first touching ground.

The other three planes made their landings in quick succession and in seven minutes from the time Plane No. 4 first touched the ground all four planes were safe on terra firma. Plane No. 1 with Captain Streett aboard was the last machine to land.

On this trip Captain Streett has always been the last one to land and the last one to take off.

Plane No. 4 has made the first landing at each stop and has also been the first one to take off from each field.

Moving Pictures Taken

Richard Suratt, representing the Fox News Agency was on the field with a moving picture camera and secured some excellent pictures which will be on the screen in New York and other eastern cities within two or three weeks.

Rev. H. P. Corser and Mr. J. E. Worden both took pictures for outside metropolitan newspapers.

Kodaks were everywhere in evidence, and among the large number of snapshots taken were some splendid pictures.

Daring Feats by Nelson and Long

The field was wet from the recent rains, thereby causing danger of the planes overturning in landing. On this account all the machines were stopped in less than the normal time after touching ground. For the purpose of steadying the planes while landing Lieutenant Nelson and Sergeant Long both performed daring feats by climbing out of their cockpits and riding to earth on the tails of their planes.

The Mayor Extends Congratulations

As Captain Streett alighted from his machine Mayor J. G Grant stepped forward and shook hands with him, at the same time congratulating him upon the safe arrival of the air squadron on Alaskan soil. Captain Streett then introduced Mayor Grant to the other aviators.

A Souvenir From Gotham

Captain Streett delivered to J. W. Pritchett a large envelope addressed to "Editor, Sentinel, Wrangell, Alaska." On the lower left hand corner was written the following: "This envelope contains a copy of the New York Times delivered by Captain St. Clair Streett, U. S. Army, New York to Nome, Alaska, Aero Expedition." The copy of the Times enclosed was found to contain an advance story of the transcontinental flight and was published on the morning that the aviators took off from Mineola field.

After landing, the aviators lost no time in getting to work on their planes, oiling them and replenishing the supply of gasoline. It was after dark before the flyers tied their machines down and left them for the night. Arriving in Wrangell the aviators found a course dinner awaiting them at the hotel.

Congratulatory Cablegrams

At the close of the dinner Mayor Grant requested J. W. Pritchett, editor of the Wrangell Sentinel, to read two cablegrams. They were as follows:

[From the Governor]

Grant, Mayor,
Wrangell.
Had hoped to get to Wrangell to greet Army aviators, but find I am unable to leave. Express my welcome and the welcome of the Territory to Captain Streett and his daring companions, and wish them every success in their trip to Nome.
RIGGS,
Governor.

[From the Mayor of Juneau]

J. O. Grant, Mayor,
Wrangell.
Please extend on behalf of the citizens of the Capital City of Alaska a hearty greeting to the gallant aviators who are making their entry into Alaska through your city and a cordial invitation to fly over our city and Gastineau channel where six thousand Alaskans are eager to see their flight.
R. E. Robertson,
Mayor.

Streett Promises to Fly Over Juneau

Captain Streett authorized Mayor Grant to inform Mayor Robertson that he would be greatly pleased to grant his request, and that he regretted that it would not be possible for the planes to make a landing at the Alaskan capital.

Thinks Worst Part of Flight is Over

Captain Streett then made a few remarks expressing his great satisfaction at landing on Alaskan soil. He said he most sincerely appreciated the kind words he and his companions had received since their arrival, but that he did not feel that any praise was really merited until they had reached Nome. He said that ever since landing here he had felt himself in an atmosphere of friendliness, and that it was perhaps the result of the good will and encouragement of the people of this town of the far north that he now had the feeling that the worst part of the flight was over and that the remainder of the trip would be down hill. He was positive that a coast hydroplane service is entirely feasible and would prove of incalculable benefit to Alaska.

Praise for McLaughlin

Lieutenant Ross Kirkpatrick said that the biggest boon they had had since leaving New York was Sergeant W. W. McLaughlin of Wrangell. Other officers applauded at the mention of Sergeant McLaughlin's name. As an advance officer of this special aero expedition Sergeant McLaughlin was a huge success. He made all arrangements beforehand and anticipated every possible requirement.

U. S. Cable Out of Commission

Sunday morning the aviators left the Wrangell hotel early for the field on Sergeif island. The weather was not altogether favorable here. Unfortunately the cable was out of commission between Juneau and Skagway. Sergeant W. W. McLaughlin of the U. S. Signal corps did everything possible to get into communication with Whitehorse by radio via Cordova, Fairbanks and other points, but all his efforts were in vain.

Take-off Postponed Till Monday

After waiting until noon trying to get a report on the weather conditions at Whitehorse, Captain Streett announced that the flight to Whitehorse would not be undertaken until the next day.

Early Monday morning the flyers left the hotel again for the field on Sergeif island. Owing to heavy rains last week the field was not in the most satisfactory condition. At 11 o'clock Captain Streett went up in Plane No. 1 to take a look at the weather. After flying high for a few minutes he considered the weather all right. He could easily have signalled this fact and have set out for Whitehorse, but he preferred to land again and see his companions off safely before he left. Upon landing he announced that the planes would undertake to hop off at 12 o'clock.

Three Planes Get Away

At 12:07 Plane No. 4 made a successful take-off. Plane No. 2 then undertook to take off and skidded into a slough. Only very slight damage resulted, but there was necessarily some delay.

Lieutenant Ross Kirkpatrick, piloting Plane No. 4 circled over the field while waiting for his companions. After being in the air 23 minutes he started out on the flight north alone, leaving at 12:30. At 1:32 Plane No. 3, piloted by Lieutenant C. H. Crumrine, made a successful take off. Two minutes later Plane No. 2, piloted by Lieutenant Clifford C. Nutt, made a good take off.

Captain Streett then attempted to take-off. His machine skidded into a slough, breaking a propeller. That meant that he would not get away that day. Mayor Grant and others took their coats off and placed themselves at Captain Streett's orders. The machine was rolled back to a solid place on the field. The broken propeller was removed, and a new one, which was on hand for an emergency was put in its place. At 6 o'clock Captain Streett and Sergeant Henriques returned to town. They both retired early and were up for breakfast before 5 o'clock Tuesday morning. At 6 o'clock they left for the field on Sergeif island, arriving there within an hour.

Capt. Streett Makes Perfect Take-off

At 8:50 Captain Streett made a beautiful take-off, getting away without the slightest difficulty. Before noon word came over the wire that Captain Streett had passed over Juneau at 10:30, flying at a considerable height.

Planes Fly Over Juneau

While on their flight northward from Wrangell the flyers went a little out of their way to give the inhabitants of the Alaskan capital a few thrills. Lieutenant Ross Kirkpatrick, piloting Plane No. 4 flew over Juneau at 2:32 Monday. He flew so low at one point that it looked as if he were going to land in the street near Goldstein's store. He dropped a gaily decorated package addressed to Governor Riggs. The package had been sent by the New York Times. An hour later Planes Nos. 2 and 3 flew over Juneau at a considerable height. At 3:33 Lieutenant Kirkpatrick was flying over the town of Skagway. From Skagway he seemed to follow the direction of the White Pass & Yukon railroad. Captain Streett, piloting Plane No. 1 flew over Juneau Tuesday forenoon.

It was the original plan to take the Governor's package to Nome and mail it to him from there, but after the invitation of Mayor Robertson to fly over Juneau was accepted, it was decided to drop the package while flying over the capital city.

Personnel of the Expedition

This is the personnel of the expedition:

Plane 1—Captain St. Clair Streett, pilot and commanding officer of the expedition; Sergeant Edmond Henriques, observer and mechanic.

Plane 2—First Lieutenant Clifford C. Nutt, second in command, pilot; Second Lieutenant Eric H. Nelson, engineering officer, pilot.

Plane 3—Second Lieutenant C. H. Crumrine, photographic officer, pilot and observer; Sergeant James Long, pilot, mechanic.

Plane 4—Second Lieutenant Ross Kirkpatrick, information officer and pilot; M. E. Sergeant Joseph E. English, mechanic and observer.

NOTES

All of the flyers but one have mothers living.

• • •

Four of the eight aviators are Southerners.

• • •

Two of aviators are foreign born. Lieutenant Eric H. Nelson is a native of Sweden, and Sergeant Edmond Henriques is a native of Australia.

• • •

The aviators decided their mascot was a hoodoo. At Edmonton they gave away a bull pup that they had brought from New York.

• • •

In the flight from Hazelton to Wrangell the aviators flew over much virgin country which on account of its inaccessibility had never before been beheld by human eyes.

• • •

One of the aviators is an acquaintance of Miss Irene Sornberger, daughter of Wesley Sornberger of Wrangell. The young people were classmates at Columbia University.

• • •

Much of the time since leaving Saskatoon the flyers have had to rely entirely on their compasses, thus putting their ability as aerial navigators to a most thorough test.

• • •

The aviators are all young men. There is only one in the party over 27 years of age. The youngest is only 22. But determination and pluck are plainly indicated in the physiognomies of all of them.

• • •

It does not look as though an air mail service would be successful in the north if single planes were used for long flights. But with a system of relays it would be possible to send a letter to Seattle today and receive an answer tomorrow.

• • •

Mayor R. H. Robertson and Hon. Charles A. Garfield of Juneau were in Wrangell a few minutes Monday evening. Upon learning that Captain Streett was in the city they called upon him at the Wrangell hotel to pay their respects.

• • •

The aviators took a number of important pictures while in flight over the inaccessible regions between Wrangell and Hazelton. Lieutenants Nelson and Nutt have had a special course of training at the Air Service School of Aerial Photography at Langley field near Hampton, Va.

• • •

Captain St. Clair Streett and Sergeants Henriques and Long saw service overseas during the war. Some of the other members of the expedition who are also excellent aviators were retained on this side during the war much against their own wishes, because their services were needed as instructors in aviation schools.

• • •

Very few people remained in town on Saturday afternoon, but those who did saw the planes first. The squadron passed over the "back channel" flying at an altitude of 6000 feet. The Wrangellites, viewing the planes from an angle, supposed they were flying low, and almost directly over Mt. Dewey.

• • •

Before leaving Hazelton Captain Streett decorated his plane with two small flags—one Canadian and one American. The American flag was lost in flight. W. Scott Simpson, Indian agent at Telegraph Creek, B. C., fell heir to the Canadian emblem and is very proud of being the possessor of the first Canadian flag that was ever brought across the Alaskan boundary in the air.

• • •

The aviators flew at an altitude of 10,000 feet part of the way from Hazelton, but greatest part of the distance between the two towns was covered at an altitude of 9000 feet. This was the highest flying done on the trip prior to reaching Wrangell. Most of the flying since leaving New York has been at an altitude of 5000 feet.

• • •

Captain Streett would make a good "Sourdough." When he finds he has ice fields and glaciers to cross he adopts the northern style of dress just as naturally as if he had always lived here. At Edmonton he bought a waterproofed coat having a fur collar and lined with lambskin with the wool not removed. At Wrangell he bought a pair of logger's rubber packs and a pair of socks that would weigh almost as much as an ordinary pair of shoes.

• • •

On Tuesday morning Captain Streett and Sergeant Henriques found that raspberries and cream were on their menu. When told that the raspberries were home grown and that there were quantities of the same luscious berries throughout the town, Capt. Street said:

"When I was flying over the continuous chain of glaciers and snow fields between here and Hazelton I never dreamed that upon reaching Wrangell it would be my privilege to feast on home grown berries and cream. The rank growth of vegetation and the beautiful flowers here seem wonderful to me."

• • •

During the war, Captain St. Clair Streett was a comrade of G. B. Lycan of Kalispell, Montana, who is a brother of Mrs. H. L. Rowley of Wrangell. The two young men enlisted at the same time—went overseas together—were together in Coblens, Germany, and returned home together.

• • •

Saturday was not the first time that Sergief Island has come into prominence in the history of the North. During the days of the Cassiar stampede, hundreds of men were camped there, preparatory to going up the Stikine River. Later, during the early Klondike rush, hundreds arrived at the island. Many of the latter party came to grief in the interior.

• • •

It is unfortunate that some of the press agencies got the wrong impression and gave out the report that the flyers would be in Alaska within three days after leaving New York. It is understood that the War Department calculated that it would take 45 days to make the round trip. This is a pioneer scouting expedition in which the government is concerned in blazing a trail, with no thought of a speed record.

• • •

The air squadron for this special international transcontinental flight consists of four De-Haviland 4-B Liberty airplanes. The four planes are not quite uniform in weight, but the average weight is about 4450 pounds.

The Liberty motors used are 420 horsepower and are equipped with an intake manifold stack.

In order to minimize the danger from fire, in case of a back fire from any of the cylinders which might ignite the gasoline in the carburetor, the intake stack affords an outlet over the top of the engine for the flame and prevents loose gasoline deposited on the engine from catching fire.

Waiting for the planes. WM, P80.12.450

Planes flying over the town of
Wrangell. WM, P80.12.449.01 AND P80.12.449.02

Kirkpatrick was the first to land on
Sergief Island on Aug. 14. His was the
first aircraft to land in Alaska from
outside its borders. WM, P80.12.448.01

The first plane to land
in Alaska. Aug. 14. 1920

All four planes on Sergief Island.
WM, P80.12.448.04 AND P97.002.001

Some of the crewmen and
townspeople from Wrangell
on Sergeif Island. WM, P80.12.452

Leaving Sergeif Island after the arrival of the planes on Barrington Transportation Company's *Hazel B No. 3.* WM, P80.12.155

WM, P97.002.002

One of the planes taking off from Sergief Island on Aug. 16 for the next leg to Whitehorse. RAA

On Aug. 16, 1920, history was made when Lieutenant Kirkpatrick in Plane No. 4 piloted the first airplane over Alaska's capital city of Juneau. He was on his way from Wrangell and Whitehorse. AHL, PCA 56-108, ROSS KIRKPATRICK COLL. AND AHL, PCA 87-1089, WINTER & POND

To Whitehorse

The next leg of the trip would take the expedition back into Canada, to Whitehorse, Yukon, 315 miles to the north. On Aug. 15, the crew went to Sergief Island to take off, but due to unfavorable weather conditions, it was decided to wait until the 16th.

At 12:07 on the 16th, Plane No. 4 made a successful takeoff. Plane No. 2 skidded into a slough with slight damage, but later took off without trouble. Plane No. 3 also took off successfully. Streett was the last to leave, and his plane also skidded into a slough and broke its propeller. Luckily a replacement had been stockpiled at Wrangell, and it was installed. It was too late to leave, so another night was spent in town.

The other three planes made a detour over Juneau, where Kirkpatrick dropped a package addressed to Gov. Thomas Riggs. He flew low over South Franklin Street at 2:32 p.m. and dropped the parcel on the roof of the Brunswick Rooms on Ferry Way. It was delivered to the governor right away. The package, now in the Alaska State Museum, contained a copy of the *New York Times*. From Juneau, the three planes flew over Skagway and followed the tracks of the White Pass & Yukon Route over White Pass and into Whitehorse.

Streett left at 8 a.m. the next morning and flew low over the Stikine River, past the Taku Glacier and above Juneau. The clouds hung low, and he was forced to fly under 1,000 feet except over the 3,000-foot White Pass, where he had scarcely 100 feet between the ground and the cloud cover.

Many people were at the landing field on a bench above the town to greet the airmen. This was the first time airplanes had flown into the Yukon Territory.

Plane No. 4 parked in Whitehorse, Yukon. YA, #6058, HARBOTTE FAMILY COLL.

An Address of Welcome

From the citizens of Whitehorse, Yukon, to Captain St. Clair Street [sic], with Sergeant Edmund Henriques; Lieutenant Clifford C. Nutt, with Lieutenant Erich Nelson; Lieutenant G.H. Crumrine, with Sergeant Long; Lieutenant Ross Kirkpatrick, with Master Electrician J.K. English, who have flown from New York and are now on their way to Nome.

DEAR FRIENDS AND NEIGHBORS:

We most heartily congratulate you in being the first airmen to fly in the Yukon territory, and especially so because you have accomplished a journey of some thousands of miles over a course traversed by no other aviators.

We are glad to know that your progressive country foresees the great future commercial usefulness of the aeroplane and that your government intends to expend $60,000,000 on aeroplanes during 1921.

We fell sure that aviation will further the comfort and convenience of the world at large and promote international good-will between your country and ours. Such a journey as yours will be the means of producing and fostering public belief in the resources of the air and give confidence to mankind that the aeroplane can be safely employed either for pleasure of for business.

We wish you a safe journey to Nome and a speedy return and rest assured that we shall ever remember the brave and intrepid men who dared to be the pioneer airmen to Yukon.

We are, with congratulations, your admiring friends:

THE CITIZENS OF WHITEHORSE

Whitehorse Star
August 20

Red Letter Day in Yukon's History

On Saturday last it became known that the American aeroplanes, which were flying from Mineola to Nome, had arrived at Wrangell, and on Sunday many people in Whitehorse ascended the hill to the west of town and waited on the aerodome with expectant eyes turned to the southeast hoping to see the planes emerge from the ethereal blue of the cloudless sky.

But the watchers returned home disappointed when supper time came round.

On Monday, however, news was received by wire that one of the planes had passed Skagway, and like a forest fire rapidly spread over the town and there was a great stampede to the landing ground.

Some on foot, some on wagons and autos rapidly ceasing their work, hastened to take up their positions so as not to miss seeing the landing of the first aeroplane on Yukon soil.

They had not long to wait before a tiny speck like a little bird could be seen coming rapidly nearer and apparently growing larger with surprising rapidity; then a deep bass musical note was heard comparable to the rich sonorous fundamental sound emitted by a great organ pipe.

The deep hum almost before we could realize it was sounding directly above our heads, then the great dragon-fly as if in joyous exultation of having caused so much excitement among the earth-bound mortals, gracefully circled about as if to show its wonderful capabilities and mastery of the air. Then, as if satisfied, it gracefully flew closely to the ground and in a few seconds had come to rest amid clouds of dust.

Then two others appeared, one on each side of the river; again the circling maneuvers were repeated until the pilots were convinced that they could safely land.

The pioneers of the air looked tired and bore anxious faces, characteristic of men who endure great mental strains, but soon looked happy when the onlookers gave them a joyous welcome.

But there was still another to come and everybody was anxious to know if all were well with Capt. Street and Observing Sergeant Henriques.

It was learned that these aviators had had difficulties in landing on muddy ground at Wrangell and would arrive the next day, Tuesday, the memorable 17th of August, Discovery Day.

On Tuesday there was another rush of people to the aerodome when it was known that Captain Street was expected to land here at about noon.

Rousing cheers were given as the commander of the expedition guided by the great white cross spread out in the center of the field and by the smoke ascending closse by, swooped down with great speed immediately above the long arm of the cross and came to rest a few yards from the spot where he first touched terra firma.

Then three cheers burst from the crowd as the captain, smiling and happy, stepped from his cramped quarters and shook hands with the excited assembly, many of whom were old-timers of Yukon and had never seen an aeroplane before....

The rudder of Plane No. 3 showing all the stops along the way from New York to Nome, Alaska. Notice that the unscheduled stop at the Twin Cities is not recorded. The plane is parked at Whitehorse, Yukon. YA, #6057, HARBOTTE FAMILY COLL. AND RAA

This letter, written on Aug. 18, 1920, to G.P. MacKenzie, Commissioner of the Yukon, urges the government to establish regular air service to the Yukon. It is signed by over 60 citizens of Whitehorse. YA

31903

Whitehorse
Yukon
o'clock Aug 18 ~~July~~

CORRESPONDENCE REGISTRATION BRANCH DAWSON
1920 AUG 21

To
The Honorable G.P. Mackenzie
Commissioner of Yukon.

Dear Sir:-

We, the citizens of Whitehorse, send you greeting by the first aeroplanes ~~which has~~ flown in Yukon.

On this historical occasion we wish to express a fervent hope that our Government will keep pace with other countries in the establishment of a regular aeroplane service throughout our Dominion and especially in Yukon where it is so much needed.

The world is cognizant of the bravery, skill and ability displayed by the Canadian Air Force in handling their machines during the Great War, so there is no dearth of competent Canadian airmen; neither is there any difficulty in obtaining suitable spruce which will ably stand the stress put upon struts and wing-beams for we have in British Columbia over 13,700 million board feet of the finest spruce in the world!

Our Yukon climate is suitable; aerodromes can be

2

easily established; Canada possesses
up-to-date aeroplanes fitted
with the most modern appliances,
therefore we hope soon to see
mail-bags substituted for bombs
and a regular service of
aeroplanes flying between
Dawson, Whitehorse and
other parts of Yukon.

Our neighbors have just
celebrated the second anniversary
of their aerial mail-service,
and have demonstrated beyond
doubt that such a service is
quicker and cheaper than
train-service. Flying postmen
in the U.S.A. last year carried
538,734 lbs weight of mail
over a mileage of 498,664 at a
saving of over $51,000.

In Great Britain passengers,
mail and parcels are safely
carried many times daily; and
owing to the marvellous
developments in wireless telephony
pilots are no longer afraid
of foggy weather

We believe that steps
should be taken immediately
to inaugurate an air-service for
Yukon which for the most part
is without railways and other
modes of rapid inter communication
We are, Dear Sir

Planes at the Whitehorse Airfield, presently the Whitehorse Airport site. RAA

To Dawson

The next leg of the journey would cost the expedition an extra day. The target for Aug. 17 was Dawson City, the capital of the Yukon Territory and once the greatest gold mining center of the world. It lay 250 miles to the northwest, and the route covered mountains, streams and moraines left by a receding glacier. As Streett later wrote in his article, "The land seems to have been dug up by a gigantic plow, the furrows running north and south."

The plan was for all four planes to arrive in Dawson on Aug. 17, exactly 24 years after the first discovery of gold in the Klondike area. For years the people of Dawson had celebrated this historic event, and on this day in 1920, people gathered at Minto Park, south of Dawson, to join the Yukon Order of Pioneers.

However, only Nutt and Kirkpatrick arrived. Crumrine was the third to take off but blew a tire and had to stop. Streett waited for Crumrine to make repairs and try another takeoff. Unfortunately, the tire burst again and a new one could only be obtained from Wrangell.

Crumrine decided to try and fix his tire in Whitehorse instead of waiting for days to obtain a new one, but so much time had been lost, that he was unable to takeoff until the next day. He simply wound rope and strips cut from a leather harness around the rim of the wheel and placed the casing over it. He landed in Dawson without incident.

When Nutt and Kirkpatrick were spotted, the people rushed to the ferry landing at the foot of Queen Street. Everyone wanted to get on the ferry to cross the Yukon River to get to Faulkner's Field, on the west side of the river. The landing area was only a hayfield on a sloping hillside.

Streett and Crumrine arrived the following day, but not without some anxious moments. Crumrine came in high over the Yukon River and landed safely in the hayfield.

But Streett was flying low, not more than 100 feet above the river, because the weather had changed and a gray overcast hung over the river valley. He did not know that a cable was stretched across the river. It ran from a tower at the foot of Queen Street to an anchorage in the rock on the opposite shore. It was used to shuttle freight, passengers, horses and equipment across the river.

Captain Streett saw it in the nick of time. He keeled over on one wing, dipped under the cable and landed safely on the hayfield. As he climbed out of his plane he stated: "The was the closest call I've ever had in my life, another second or two and our plane would have been cut in half."

The squadron left for Fairbanks the next day. On their return trip, all four planes landed in Dawson on Sept. 1. A ball was held that night at the Arctic Brotherhood Hall in their honor. The fliers were inducted into the Yukon Order of Pioneers.

View of the tire Crumrine repaired in Whitehorse. RAA

Royal Northwest Mounted Police in front of Plane No. 2. RAA

All four planes at Faulkner's Field in West Dawson. YA, #9411, CLAYTON BETTS COLL.

Crumrine arriving at Faulkner's Field on Aug. 18 from Whitehorse. RAA

Dawson in 1920 was still a major gold mining center but its population was only a fraction of what it had been in 1898 at the height of the gold rush. RAA

To Fairbanks

After a tremendous welcome in Dawson and a tour of the historic goldfields, now being eaten up by huge gold dredges, the expedition was ready for a 275-mile flight back into Alaska on one of its last legs to Nome.

On the morning of Aug. 19, the four planes were winging their way across trackless miles of tundra to the goldrush town of Fairbanks. Late in the afternoon, all four planes arrived over the city, landed at Exposition Park and pulled up near the grandstand. Captain Douglas had arranged for supplies to be stocked in Fairbanks and minor repairs were made to the planes, including installing a new tire on Crumrine's aircraft.

By this time, the airmen were used to large enthusiastic crowds, and the people of Fairbanks were no exception. As Fairbanks was only 120 miles south of the Arctic Circle and was connected to the outside world only by a long railroad and highway to tidewater, the arrival of the airplanes gave its citizens hope that regular air service would soon be initiated. They could not believe it had only taken 50 hours of flying time to reach their city from New York. After flying over miles and miles of bleak and forbidding country, the airmen could not get over the verdant, abundant crops and beautiful flower gardens in Fairbanks and the Tanana Valley. This after flying over miles and miles of bleak and forbidding country.

After speeches, meals and a dance at the armory that night, the expedition was ready for the next-to-last leg to Nome the next morning.

Axel Carlstet was the fliers host in Fairbanks.
RAA

Ads were placed in the paper every day for the big aviation ball scheduled for the day the fliers arrived.

Fairbanks Daily News-Miner

AND THE DAILY ALASKA CITIZEN

18TH YEAR   FAIRBANKS, ALASKA, FRIDAY, AUGUST 13, 1920.   WHOLE NUMBER 5241

THE FLIERS ARE HEADED THIS WAY ONCE MORE

War Is Worse and More of It As the Hours Pass

FLYERS ARE STARTING

Prince George to Hazelton 9

DUE TONIGHT

Hazelton to Wrangell, Alaska ..21

SATURDAY NIGHT

Wrangell to White Horse

SUNDAY NIGHT

White Horse to Dawson

MONDAY NIGHT

Dawson to Fairbanks

WHEN THEY ARRIVE

PRINCE GEORGE, Aug. 13.—(Delayed) The New York to Nome aviators plan to leave here tomorrow and reach Hazelton tomorrow night (this night)

STILL EXPECTING SOMETHING EVEN AS YOU AND I

PRINCE GEORGE, B. C., Aug. 13.—The army aviators expect to get away for Hazelton before night

GREEK MET ASSASSIN

PARIS, Aug. 13.—An attempt was made last evening to assassinate Premier Venizelos of Greece.

An attack upon the Premier was made at the Lyons railway station. Two of the bullets fired at him struck him, one in the shoulder and one in the side, but from early reports of his injuries the wounds are not believed to be serious.

CABBAGE, large sound heads, 10c pound. John Scharis.

Everybody Is Fighting For Protection Of Poor Poland

PARIS, Aug. 13.—General Weygand, assistant to Marshal Foch, has been offered supreme command of the Polish forces.

A week ago this noted warrior announced that he would accept the command of the Polish forces if it was offered him, and that he didn't consider the Polish situation hopeless by any measure.

GAVE 'EM THE STEEL

WARSAW, Aug. 13. The Poles launched a counter attack with bayonets against the Bolsheviki in the region of Pultusk, thirty miles north of here.

The Russian cavalry has reached Praga.

The Polish peace delegates left yesterday to meet the Russian delegates at Minsk.

WE ARE IN IT

WASHINGTON, Aug. 13.—The pre-

direction credited here that a result of the Wilson note will be the reimposition of an embargo on trade with Soviet Russia.

ONE GOOD FIGHTING PEOPLE

WARSAW, Aug. 13.—Yesterday the Poles launched a counter-offensive attack against the Russians in the region of Pultusk, where the Russians are striving to break the Polish defensive lines.

Hundreds of conveyances loaded with barbed wire and driven by boys and old men are streaming thru the Polish capital toward the battle front, and mingled with them are endless trains of supply wagons guarded by elderly civilians armed with rifles.

All the able-bodied men in this section of Poland have been relieved from other duties so that they may fight for the defense of Warsaw.

Women soldiers are acting and of Warsaw, according to a wireless message received here today from Berlin.

BRITISH FLEET MOVING

LONDON, Aug. 13.—A fleet of British battleships bound for the Russian coast having left Danish waters was sighted off Utrecht yesterday.

WILD RIDERS OF THE PLAINS

LONDON, Aug. 13.—The Russian cavalry has reached Praga, a suburb

BURLESON HIS FRIEND

BOSTON, Aug. 13.—Charles Ponzi last evening surrendered to the United States Marshal on the charge of using the United States mail to defraud.

His liabilities are $7,000,000 and he claims to have assets of $4,000,000, all made in speculating in foreign exchange.

NEW ENGLANDERS FELL

BOSTON, Aug. 13.—Developments to date indicate that Ponzi induced 10,000 New Englanders to invest $70,000,000 in fraudulent schemes for the purchase of foreign exchange.

STEPPED ON BABE'S KNEE

CLEVELAND, Aug. 13.—Babe Ruth was forced to retire from yesterday's game when he dislocated his knee while sliding to second base in the first inning, but he will probably be back in the game today.

He tried to continue playing after his injury was sustained, but collapsed and had to be carried from the field.

BACK IN THE HARNESS

CLEVELAND, Aug. 13.—Babe Ruth wearing an elastic knee bandage played in yesterday afternoon's game with Cleveland.

There is no injury to the knee bone and no ligaments are torn.

OLD MEXICO TREMBLED

MEXICO CITY, Aug. 13.—Earthquake tremblers which lasted for 35 minutes were detected by the seismograph in the government observatory here last evening.

WANT TO GET TOGETHER

LONDON, Aug. 13.—The church conference at Lambeth urges the union of all kinds of churches in one great church, and appeals to all christian people to aid in bringing about this desired end.

(Good idea—the "overhead" would cost less and the various routes to hell be restricted to one main traveled road.)

R. BOYKER PINCH'D AGAIN

SEATTLE, Aug. 13.—Early this morning the police again raided the Northern hotel, seized a large quantity of whiskey secreted there and arrested Ralph Boyker, the proprietor of the joint.

GIRLS WIN AFTER ALL

NASHVILLE, Aug. 13.—The Tennessee senate today voted by 25 to 4 to ratify the woman suffrage amendment to the Constitution.

The final ratification, however, is not possible this week, as the house adjourned this afternoon until Monday next.

MORE WAR DOPE COMES

FRANCE IS PLEASED

PARIS, Aug. 13.—The French government is sending a note to President Wilson expressing pleasure that the French and American views on the Russo-Polish situation are in complete accord.

IN STATE OF SIEGE

WARSAW, Aug. 13.—The Russian Soviet forces have penetrated to a point within 25 miles of Warsaw and a state of siege has been declared here by the military governor of Warsaw. Civilians are not permitted to be on the streets after dark, an other siege orders are in force.

UKRAINIA ON HER DIGNITY

VIENNA, Aug. 13.—Ukrainia has

IN ALL BUT ONE THING

MARION, O., Aug. 13.—Governor Cox passing thru this city this morning sent Candidate Harding word that he wished him good luck "in everything but one thing."

THE DENVER CAR STRIKE

DENVER, Aug. 13.—Explosives placed under the rails on the streets car track last night on Stout Street damaged the track and crippled a car today, and the police declare it to be the work of striking street car men.

James McPike of Gilmore creek came in for a few days. He reports

Fairbanks Daily News-Miner
AND THE DAILY ALASKA CITIZEN

18TH YEAR — 14   FAIRBANKS, ALASKA THURSDAY, AUGUST 19, 1920.   WHOLE NUMBER 5216

THE SKIES OF THE HEART OF ALASKA ARE FILLED WITH AIRSHIPS

Mail Delivered From Dawson Today In 2 Hours 20 Min.

THE OLD HUNTER IS REOPENED

AND THE NIGHT WILL BE FILLED WITH MUSIC

HUNTING STORY AS IT IS TOLD

WARNING TO THE PUBLIC IN REGARD TO

AIRCRAFT

WHEN AN AEROPLANE IS ON THE GROUND

DON'T crowd round the machine — for just what it must be doing.

DON'T touch any part of the aeroplane or you may mistake — get the propeller. Do what he asks you at once.

DON'T smear or throw liquid anti-rust while of the machine, as it may be dangerous petrol fumes about.

WHEN AN AEROPLANE IS LANDING OR RISING

DON'T run to where you think it will land. Keep out of the way, near a fence or other obstacle, and wait until it stops.

DON'T stand in the direct run of an airplane which is about to rise.

DON'T let children or animals stray in the route of a landing or rising airplane.

BIG DANCE AT THE ARMORY TONIGHT

THE CITY OF FAIRBANKS IS HOST TONIGHT AT A BIG AVIATORS' DANCE, AT THE ARMORY, EVERYTHING FREE.

WE'RE GOING SOME

MORE MAIL FOR US

NOT A RACING PLAY

AND, EVERYBODY'S HEADY

GETTING OFF EASY

ACTUAL FLYING TIME

UNKINDEST CUT OF ALL

KEEP OFF THE GROUND

NOTICE—IMPORTANT

Crumrine christened his plane *Nordic*. As a newspaper article mentioned, he had been pronounced by the chief psychological officer at Carlstrom Field in Florida to be a perfect Nordic type, having light hair, fair complexion and blue eyes. The article also stated that Army records showed that men of this type made the most daring fighters. RAA

Lieutenant Crumrine in the front seat with his dog, "Nordic," and Lieutenant Nelson with his dogs, "Nome" and "Sister," given to the fliers by the citizens of Fairbanks. RAA

Captain Douglas (center) pictured with several crewmen and their new pets. CAM

The crews were taken out on a duck hunt in the Fairbanks area. This photo shows Lieutenant Nutt. RAA

The four planes lined up on the field at Exposition Park.
AMHA B76.14.52

Fairbanks Daily News-Miner
AND THE DAILY ALASKA CITIZE

18TH YEAR 13   FAIRBANKS, ALASKA, FRIDAY, AUGUST 20, 1920.   WHOLE NUMBER 5347

THE FLYERS CAME AND DEPARTED AND WE ARE STILL HERE

POLAND IS RECOGNIZED

LONDON, Aug 20 — The Russian ace delegates at Minsk have been instructed to recognize fully the national existence of Poland and to interfere in domestic affairs of that country, says a Minsk dispatch to the ...

ARE FIGHTING ONCE AGAIN

BERLIN Aug 20 — Twenty German soldiers, many civilians and thirteen French soldiers have been killed ...

BEYOND OUR IMAGINATION

MARION, O., Aug 20 Harding in his speech this afternoon said ...

THE EVENT DISRUPTED THE EVEN TENOR OF OUR WAY

POLES ARE WINNING NOW

WARSAW, Aug 20 The eighty-sixth ...

BOLSHEVIKI ARE FLEEING

WARSAW, Aug 20. The Russian Soviet forces are fleeing in a disorderly panic along the battle-front to meet the Vistula and the Bug ...

BUT TOMORROW IS ANOTHER DAY

Altho Mark Twain omitting mention of that detail, we are inclined to believe that "The Man Who Corrupted Hadleyburg" must have been of the kind; aviator, for if ever a camp was corrupted, speedily like, it was this ship, also by the arrival of the aviators ...

A BEAUTIFUL LANDING

LATER THAN THAT

WHAT'S THE USE?

POLES ARE GOING SOME

WARSAW, Aug. 20. The extreme right wing of the Polish army is marching on Brestlitovsk and has taken several towns ...

THEY'RE UP AGAINST IT

CONSTANTINOPLE, Aug. 20.— ... Turkish bullets and facing starvation, 18 American workers in the American Commission for relief in the near east, have been besieged in Adana, Asia Minor, since June 20th ...

Jim Hagen, Deputy U. S. Marshal at Nenana, came to Fairbanks for the arrival of the airplanes.

BLACK HOUSE IS FOR HIM

NEW YORK, Aug. 20—The Universal Negro improvement society in convention here announced that a leader of the fifteen million negroes in the United States would be elected president of that society next Thursday night ...

GOVER'MENTS IN ACCORD

WASHINGTON, D. C., Aug. 20 — Secretary of State Colby announced today that the French reply to the American note has been received, and that the two governments are in absolute accord on non-recognition of the Russian Soviet government.

HURRAH FOR THE INDIANS

MARION, O., Aug. 20 — Senator Harding, in one of his front-porch speeches here today after recalling that the white man had taken the Indians' land, said: "I believe in the policy of promoting the ideals of Democracy in America first, and the American Indian is just as much entitled to that which rightously comes to him as any other citizen." He also declared for the conservation of American forests.

Mr. and Mrs. Tom Gilmore are spending a few days in town.

 *To Ruby and Nome*

There was a light drizzle on the morning of Aug. 20 when the four planes took off from Fairbanks' Exposition Park. The pilots had excellent U.S. Geological Survey maps to guide them down the Yukon River Valley to the remote mining town of Ruby.

Captain Douglas had arranged for a landing field on a solid gravel bar island six miles from town. The planes flew up the Tanana River Valley until Harper's Bend was reached, south of Fort Gibbons, and then entered the great Yukon River Valley. After a flight of two hours and 45 minutes over 240 miles, the planes made perfect landings at Ruby. Streett thought this sandbar strip was the best landing site of the entire trip.

The landing of the planes was such a great event for this remote site that the local natives had been gathering for days to greet them. They gave up their fishing and trapping and cleaned out the food shelves from the three local stores, so there was a threat of a drastic food shortage.

The citizens of Nome had scheduled a big celebration for the expedition on Aug. 24, the very earliest arrival date considered possible when the flight was being planned. Since the planes had landed in Ruby on the 20th, it was decided to wait there until Nome was ready for them.

The crew went out to hunt caribou and bear and to fish in the Yukon River. A local took them on a wild ride down the muddy main street in a dog sled. The natives staged a pow wow and dance in their honor.

After two days, Nome telegraphed that it was ready to receive the airmen, so on the afternoon of Aug. 23, all four planes took off smoothly from Ruby. At 5:30 p.m. they landed at the old parade ground adjoining the abandoned Fort Davis, situated between the Nome River and the Bering Sea. Walter E. Care, a World War I combat pilot, helped lay out the landing strip. Through the center of the parade ground ran a slightly curved road. The 400-yard-long strip had been oiled and was widened to a width of 100 yards.

After 39 days, 4,500 miles from Mitchel Field and 53 hours and 30 minutes of flying time, their goal was met. And all this without an engine failure or major accident. Streett wanted to make a short 150-mile hop across the Bering Sea to a landing on the continent of Asia in Siberia, but authorities in Washington, D.C., decided against it.

The captain delivered the mail carried from New York to the delight of the citizens of this remote part of Alaska. Nome could be reached only by ships for a short time in the summer months or only by a long dog sled trip in the winter. To no place else in Alaska would the airplane be of greater benefit.

The heroic crewmen were carried into Nome at the head of a parade, and a banquet was given by local American Legion members. A reception was also given by the local Arctic Brotherhood lodge, and many gifts, including a loving cup, were presented to the crew.

Ruby, Alaska. RAA

Main Street of Ruby. RAA

Ruby had only a shadow of the population it had at the height of the gold rush. RAA

A landing field was picked on the top of a hill above Ruby, but a sandbar in the river was used instead. RAA

A crowd of Ruby citizens waiting for the planes to land on the sandbar. RAA

Streett landing on the sandbar. RAA

Planes lined up for the night. RAA

THE NOME NUGGET

8 Pages

The only newspaper published on
Seward Peninsula.
Covers approximately 22,700
square miles of territory

VOLUME XXI — No. 35   NOME, ALASKA SATURDAY AUG. 28 1920.   Delivered by Carrier or Mailed......$1.00 per Month

BOLSHEVIKI ARE COMING BACK
CHAMBER COMMERCE DEMANDS LATE SAILING
ALASKAN FLYING EXPEDITION FROM NEW YORK TO NOME SUCCESSFULLY NEGOTIATES LONG JOURNEY

Four Planes Land in Nome Monday Evening: Three Hundred Mile Trip From Ruby in 3 hrs. 15 min. Flyers Given Rousing Welcome by Nome Populace

The great army air flight from New York to Nome was successfully completed Monday evening with the arrival at Nome of the four airplanes comprising the expedition shortly before 6 p. m.

Flying low to escape the heavy cloud masses filling the upper air, the planes came breaking up from the eastern horizon about 5:20 and, after passing over the town in a series of spectacular circles, swung over the landing field at Ft Davis and descended safely amid the tumultuous cheers of the crowd gathered along the west bank of Nome River opposite the landing field.

Practically everyone in the city watched the thrilling spectacle as the flyers' turned and circled above the field before swooping downward, to make their landing and cheer after cheer went up from the throng as the planes came to a halt one after the other at intervals of four or five minutes.

Plane No. 4, piloted by Lieutenant Ross Kirkpatrick, with Master Electrician Sergeant Jas. E. English as observer, was the first to touch the earth at 5:35 p. m. After swinging over the field in a series of mazy loops, the plane suddenly swooped downward from the eastern end of the field and came to a halt after a short run along the hard packed roadway running across the landing place. The descent was accomplished without the slightest difficulty and the plane taxi-

was swung around by the members of the American Legion appointed to assist the landing and taxied quickly back to the east end of the field to make way for the others. Within a few minutes plane No. 3 swung downward from the west and was followed in quick succession by the others. Plane No. 1, carrying Capt. St Clair Streett, commander of the expedition, and observer-mechanician Sergeant Edmund Henriques, was the last to leave the air.

Arrangements at the field were excellent and the flyers were given every assistance by former air service Lieutenant W. E. Case and those delegated for that purpose. No one was allowed on the field aside from the reception committee, representatives of the Marshal's office, who policed the field, the landing committee, a few photographers and a small scattering of others. Only four ladies were permitted on the landing place, three being Red Cross nurses, the other, Miss Catherine Anpher, a deputy marshal on the staff of Marshal Jordan. Former Lieutenant Case was in sole charge of the field and handled the situation with the thoroughness of long experience in the air service.

Following the landing, the flyers were given hearty welcome and the freedom of the city during their stay. The field was also thrown open to the public and the crowd soon swarmed around the planes watching the avia-

shape" before leaving them, or paused to permit themselves to be photographed or to answer the numerous questions of the eager crowd of spectators gathered around them.

The flyers were plainly pleased by the warmth of their reception and amiably submitted to the numerous introductions, handshakings and questioning to which they were subjected.

Capt. Streett informed the Nugget representative that every one of the eight members of the expedition were delighted with their success in accomplishing the long and difficult journey from the Atlantic coast.

"We consider our flight has accomplished what was believed to be im-

possible," he said.

Describing the trip across Alaska, he said the weather had been more or less unfavorable most of th way. Their passage across the States and Canada had also been beset with weather difficulties and seven days were lost before the planes reached Saskatoon, Saskatchewan. Further time was lost during their difficult and dangerous passage of the Rockies, and further delays were caused by an accident to his plane at Prince George. Leaky gas tanks on the remaining planes also retarded the expedition. The actual flying time of the ex-

(Continued on Page Two.)

Capt. Roald Amundsen, with book, and Capt. Howard Douglas at Nome in 1920. Amundsen was a famous Norwegian explorer who discovered the South Pole in 1911. He arrived in Nome on July 28, 1920, having navigated the Northwest Passage in the Arctic area between 1918 and 1920. He was lost in an airplane crash in the Arctic in 1928. RAA

The old Army post, Fort Davis, at Nome, was the only suitable landing area close to the town. RAA

On Monday, Aug. 23, the first plane came in from Ruby to land at Nome. AHL, PCA #56-116, ROSS KIRKPATRICK COLL.

Plane No. 4 at Nome. UAA #91-098-757N, KENNEDY COLL.

Residents of Nome line up in front of one of the planes. Abandoned military wagons can be seen behind the left wing. AHL, PCA 01-1007, EARLY PRINTS OF ALASKA COLL.

The airplanes parked along the white-frame buildings of abandoned Fort Davis. The Fort was the center of social life in Nome during the early 1900s. It provided the only suitable landing site close to the town. AHL, PCA #56-107, ROSS KIRKPATRICK COLL.

The crewmen after completing their historic flight to Nome. From left: Henriques, English, Long, Crumrine, Nelson, Nutt and Kirkpatrick. Streett is missing. This photograph gives a good view of the seating arrangement and Liberty motor. AC

Another view of the crewmen with the official greeting committee of Nome. The crew from left: Henriques, Long, English, Streett, Crumrine. Behind Streett, Nutt, Nelson and Kirkpatrick. AHL, PCA 56-114, ROSS KIRKPATRICK COLL.

Captain Streett's plane just before taking off from Nome. RAA

One of the planes ready for takeoff from Fort Davis. AHL

THE AIR EXPEDITION

Unless some unforseen contigency appears, before the Weekly Nugget again greets its readers Nome and the great Alaska Northland will have witnessed the consummation of one of the most momentous events in their history—The completion of the great Army airplane flight from New York to Nome.

Alaska's far spreading reaches, its mighty plains and valleys, its towering peaks will have been traversed from end to end by the latest and most wonderful devices that man has yet evolved to conquer time and distance and overcome the limitations by which Nature has bound him to the sod.

A new pathway will have been opened across a mighty wilderness over which in time to come will pass swift moving argosies of trade and commerce and pulsing life.

Viewed from the standpoint of its bearing on the future of the territory the successful completion of the great flight will be in every way of the most superlative importance.

Alaska's first air trail will have been carved and the first step been taken toward the removal of the most formidable obstacles to her growth and progress—the obstacles of mighty distances and slow transportation.

Like the first faint trails worn by those dauntless old pioneers who opened this great country to human endeavor and progress, the airy pathway cut athwart Alaska's skies by the equally dauntless men of the Army air service will become the highways of the future, the arteries through which will flow new vigor and vitality which will make the land no longer a wilderness but a home for contented and prosperous thousands.

Distance is Alaska's greatest handicap and this the airplane is able to overcome far more effectively than any other human agency. Miles which under present conditions require weeks to traverse may be easily covered in hours by those fleet winged messengers of the air and time itself is reduced to small dimensions before their space annihilating rush through the ether lanes;

Laboring under the retarding difficulties of vast distances and costly and inefficient means of transportation, the airplane represents to Alaska a welcome hope and promise of early and vast assistance in overcoming the greatest obstacles to her progress and development.

The value of the present expedition to the territory cannot be over-estimated, for it brings us to the portal of a new era of material progress whose limits are beyond the scope of human vision.

The *Nome Nugget*
August 28

The *Wrangell Sentinel*
August 26

Planes in Air Only 55 Hours New York to Nome

NOME, Aug. 24.—The four U. S. Army airplanes arrived here safely yesterday afternoon.

The trip was made from Ruby without accident, although they were delayed there for a few days by bad weather.

The actual flying time from New York to Nome was 55 hours, or less than five days of daylight flying. The distance covered is estimated at over 4,500 miles.

The aviators expect to hop off in a few days on their return trip to New York. They hope to lower both their actual flying time and the elapsed time on the trip east, as they are now familiar with the route and their machines are in excellent working order, having been thoroughly broken in on the long trip west.

It is freely predicted that the time will yet come, and will not be very long on the way either, when it will be possible to go from Nome to New York in 45 hours, actual elapsed time.

In order to make a trip of that kind it would possibly be necessary for the passengers to transfer a half dozen times on the way. One plane would carry the passengers from Nome to Fairbanks; another to Dawson, a third direct overland to Prince George, the fourth across the Rocky Mountains to Edmonton, a fifth to the vicinity of St. Paul or Chicago, and thence to New York.

It has been said that a simpler way to get from Interior Alaska to the Eastern States would be to continue due east from Dawson across the mountains to the McKenzie river country, and thence over a comparatively flat country to New York.

Airplanes Are Again Delayed

The four army airplanes took off from Nome on their return trip on Thursday, August 26. Shortly after getting into the air Captain Streett found his engine was not working properly. He returned to the field at Nome. By the time he had gotten his engine to working satisfactorily the weather had become so unfavorable that he did not deem it expedient to take off. He has been at Nome the past week waiting for fair weather. Planes Nos. 2, 3 and 4 are waiting for him at Fairbanks.

NEW YORK—The Aero Club of America today wired the aviators at Nome, congratulating them and declaring that they had given a splendid demonstration of how the most remote parts of the country can be brought in close touch with the Government. The club also predicted their achievement would be a forerunner of mail and commercial routes which the organization hopes will soon be established.

NEW YORK, Aug. 25.—News of the arrival of the army airplanes at Nome aroused much enthusiasm among the members of the Aero Club of America here. Particularly were the members elated over the fact that the aviators had made the trip over virgin country, untouched and in many places untrammeled by man, and without an accident of any consequence. The fact that it took the aviator somewhat longer than was originally anticipated did not lessen their praise for it was felt that they had pursued the wise course in studying conditions well and in using every precaution to safeguard their lives and their planes.

"It was a remarkable epoch-making achievement which foreshadows better communication facilities, not only for Alaska but for other distant lands. We shall urge the Government to establish aerial mail routes to Nome," said August Post, secretary of the club.

Crumrine's plane at Fort Davis. Notice the extensive wear on the wing surfaces. RAA

 *The Trip Home*

The trip to Nome was a success but now the planes had to return to New York. The route would be reversed and the same planes and crews would have to fight the elements, fatigue, stress and mechanical breakdowns all over again.

Captain Douglas was at Hazelton when the planes returned there. He was called back to Washington, so he took Sergeant Henriques' place as crewman on Streett's plane. Henriques returned to New York by train.

In addition, each plane had accumulated a variety of gifts and souvenirs to haul back. Two frisky sled-dog pups had been given to the crew as a farewell gift by the people of Fairbanks. They were wrapped in blankets and put in boxes set between the mechanics' legs. But they barked and chewed at everything within reach. By the time the planes left Whitehorse, the dogs had calmed down and gotten into the routine of flying.

The squadron left Nome on Aug. 31 and arrived at Ruby by dusk, then flew on to Fairbanks for a thorough check of the DH-4s. From there they flew east and south to Dawson City and Whitehorse, where they landed on Sept. 5.

By this time, fall and poor weather was imminent in the North Country so a hasty retreat from Whitehorse was ordered. But violent winds and a snowstorm forced the planes back twice, and it was not until Sept. 10 that the weather cleared enough for an inland dash south to Telegraph Creek, British Columbia.

They landed on a hayfield on the Diamond C Ranch, 12 miles down the Stikine River. Crumrine's plane was heavily damaged upon landing, and the next day Streett and Nutt took a river launch to Wrangell where they bought replacement parts.

Bad weather kept the planes grounded on the ranch until Sept. 29, when they took off for Hazelton. From there the story is sketchy, but all the planes left Hazelton and arrived in Prince George on Oct. 4, Jasper and Edmonton on Oct. 8, Saskatoon on Oct. 10, Portal and Fargo on Oct. 11, Winona on Oct. 16 (Minneapolis was overflown), Grand Rapids on Oct. 16, Erie on Oct. 18 and Mitchel Field on Oct. 20. As the four planes approached the city limits of New York, a fleet of 35 airplanes escorted them to the field. Waiting there were representatives of the War Department and several hundred spectators.

The four DH-4s and eight crewmen had covered a total of 9,329 miles in 97 days with 112 hours of flying time. The feat was managed, as Captain Streett wrote later, "with the same airplanes, the same motors, and the same spark-plugs."

The next day the squadron flew from Mitchel Field to Bolling Field, Washington, D.C., for a formal ceremony. Generals Pershing, March and Menoker were on hand to greet them. When the four planes were first sighted by scout planes, General Menoker took off in his plane to meet the squadron. He took a position immediately behind Streett's plane and landed with the squadron. General Mitchell commanded three squadrons also in the air. Each squadron consisted of 18 airplanes, flying in V-formation, making a total of 54 representing the Air Service. In addition, there were a number of civilian aircraft. Col. William H. Hensley Jr., commanding the airship, *USS Zodiac*, flew up from Langley Field with a full crew of 24 officers and men.

Thus ended a remarkable trip that opened up the airways of northwestern Canada and Alaska and proved that military and commercial aviation was a viable option in the area.

"Nome," the dog Nelson received, accompanied the crews back to New York. RAA

THE WRANGELL

VOL. XIX. NO. 38   WRANGELL, ALASKA, THURSDAY, SEPTE

Plane 4 Lands At Wrangell On Return Flight

Encounters Fog Which Is Cleared by Plane 4 In Vicinity Taku Glacier — Lands at Wrangell

Plane No. 4 made a perfect take-off from the aviation field on Sergeif island at 1:45 this afternoon. The weather here was exceptionally good for flying. A message from Hazelton reports weather perfectly clear there.

Lieut. Kirkpatrick was good enough to fly low over Wrangell after taking off.

Wrangell was thrown into excitement Thursday evening at 6:30 by the buzzing of an airplane over the dock. The plane flew so low that it was recognized as plane 4. Early in the afternoon word had been received by cable that the planes had left Whitehorse for Glenora. Under these circumstances it was only natural that the presence of plane 4 flying over Wrangell should be the signal for general excitement. Everybody was asking questions that nobody could answer. While one person was asking if all four planes had come to Wrangell another would be inquiring if there had been an accident.

Sergeant W. W. McLaughlin lost no time in hiring a boat and proceeding to the landing field. Upon his arrival there he found Lieutenant Kirkpatrick and Sergeant Joseph E. Englian in waiting.

Lieutenant Kirkpatrick reported that all four planes took off from Whitehorse that afternoon, and encountered a heavy fog. Plane 4 cleared the fog in the vicinity of Taku glacier and came to Wrangell in preference to returning to Whitehorse.

Plane 4 expected to take off for Hazelton the next morning, but owing to unfavorable atmospheric conditions did not get away until this afternoon.

On Friday planes 1, 2 and 3 took off from Whitehorse. In landing at Glenora plane 3 broke the axle of its landing gear. Captain Street immediately chartered Captain Sid Barrington's Hazel B No. 4 and came to Wrangell for repair parts for plane 3. He arrived here Saturday night, having in his company Lieutenant C. C. Nutt of plane 2. They left for Glenora Sunday afternoon.

The aviators have eight malamute dogs with them on their return flight, which will doubtless attract considerable attention in the east.

The people of Wrangell were greatly pleased at having plane 4 here a second time after having given up all hope of seeing any more planes for awhile. Several citizens decided to present Lieutenant Kirkpatrick and Sergeant English with Alaskan souvenirs before they took off for Hazelton. A beautiful Chilkat blanket was purchased for Lieutenant Kirkpatrick, while for Sergeant English the gift selected was a rare totem carved out of jet black shale. The presents were delivered to the birdmen accompanied by the following notes:

Wrangell, Alaska,
September 10, 1920.
Lieutenant Ross Kirkpatrick,
Plane No. 4
New York to Nome, Alaska
Aero Expedition

Sir:

On behalf of several citizens I present you with this Chilkat blanket, woven by Indian hands in the land of the Northern Lights. We wish you to accept this as a souvenir from Wrangell, the town where you made your first landing on Alaska soil.

We are proud of you, Lieutenant Kirkpatrick. Your dauntless courage and that of your gallant companions has made possible a glorious accomplishment which represents an epoch in our history, and the dawning of a new era in the progress and development of Alaska. It is therefore in a spirit of gratitude as well as in testimony of heroic accomplishment that this slight token is presented. We bid you Godspeed. You will ever have a warm place in our hearts.

Cordially and sincerely,
J. G. Grant, Mayor.

Wrangell, Alaska,
September 10, 1920.
Sergeant Joseph E. English,
Plane No. 4
New York to Nome, Alaska
Aero Expedition

Sir:

On behalf of several citizens I present you with this totem, the handiwork of a primitive artisan who has long since been gathered to his fathers. We wish you to accept this totem as a souvenir from Wrangell, the town where you made your first landing on Alaska soil.

We are proud of you, Sergeant English. No finer achievement is written in the annals of man's conquest of the forces of nature than this pioneer flight from the Atlantic ocean to the Bering sea. We bid you Godspeed. You will ever have a warm place in our hearts.

Cordially and sincerely,
J. G. Grant, Mayor.

The Sentinel has been fortunate in receiving mail from two different cities in opposite directions from Wrangell. The following letter from Nome was delivered in Wrangell on the return flight:

Nome, Alaska,
August 25, 1920.
Mr. J. W. Pritchett,
Editor Wrangell Sentinel,
Wrangell, Alaska.

Greetings: To you and the people of your vicinity from the Nome Nugget, Nome, Alaska, via Army Pioneer Air Expedition, to and through the land of the midnight sun, blazing the first air trail across the continent from the Bering sea to the Atlantic ocean.

Nome Nugget
Per Geo. S. Maynard,
Publisher.

Mayor J. G. Grant of Wrangell is sending a letter to Mayor John Hylan of New York by air route which will be delivered by Lieutenant Kirkpatrick.

Plane 4 will also carry a letter from the publisher of the Sentinel to the publisher of the New York Times. Through the great courtesy of Lieutenant Kirkpatrick this letter will be delivered by him personally in New York. It reads as follows:

Wrangell, Alaska,
September 10, 1920.
Mr. Adolph S. Ochs,
Publisher New York Times,
New York City.

Dear Sir:

The letter which you were good enough to send me by Captain St. Clair Streett was delivered promptly upon the arrival here of the New York to Nome Aero Expedition.

You have made me your debtor, for I am very happy to have the distinction of having received the first letter ever brought from the States to Alaska by airplane.

The feasibility of an air route to Alaska having become an established fact it is now the hope of the long-suffering public of this northern dependency that a regular air mail service may soon be established between Alaska and the States. At present our mail comes by freight, and is not hurried along any more than any other cargo.

Being one of the heaviest consumers of print paper in the United States you are naturally interested in the paper situation, and fully appreciate the argument used for an abundant supply of print paper that is offered for sale at a price somewhat cheaper than linen or silk.

The natural resources of Southeastern Alaska are well adapted to the needs of the paper industry. With her enormous forests of rapidly growing species suitable for pulp, her water power, her lime deposits, her tidewater shipment of manufactured products, Alaska should become one of the principal paper sources of the United States.

It is only during the last few months that the Bureau of Forestry has been making any real effort toward bringing about the development of this great resource. Recent Government estimates indicate that Alaska has pulp resources in excess of any section of the United States. It is estimated that the Tongrass Forest reserve alone could easily furnish over a million tons of paper products yearly, and could continue to supply indefinitely one-third to one-half of the present paper requirements of the entire country.

The Wrangell sawmill is this week cutting lumber for Alaska's first paper mill, which is being built at Port Snettisham. The reason Alaska has not had paper mills sooner is because the Federal law have been so unfavorable, both as to timber leases and water rights; that little encouragement could be offered for the investment of capital along that line. However, Congress has recently removed the main obstacles, and pulp industries for Alaska may now be installed with the assurance that they will be protected. Therefore, I am confident that the paper mill now being built will be followed by others. I expect at no distant date to read the New York Times and other leading papers of the country with a thrill of pride in knowing that the paper on which they are printed was manufactured in Southeastern Alaska.

Fraternally,
J. W. Pritchett.

Last Friday Forest Supervisor C. H. Flory of Ketchikan wired Capt. St. Clair Streett at Whitehorse requesting that if possible he fly up the Unuk river in an effort to locate 12 lost members of the international boundary survey crew who are over-due and whom it is feared have been wrecked in a 30-foot polling boat. Superintendent Flory thought that if the men are still alive the airplanes might be able to locate their camp. Captain Streett immediately wired Flory that he would grant his request. Captain Streett then wired orders to Lieutenant Kirkpatrick at Wrangell to make a flight up the Unuk river while en route from Wrangell to Hazelton. Flory stated in his message to Streett that he was starting a searching party up the river in a boat.

Close-up view of the three fliers. UAA #91-098-256N, KENNEDY COLL.

This photo was signed by Eric Nelson in 1960, 40 years after his famous flight. Kirkpatrick (left) and Nutt (right), are eating and drinking coffee while Nelson holds his new dog, "Nome," which he received in Nome. They are in Fairbanks on their return flight. In August 1947, General Nelson revisited Nome to speak to the Chamber of Commerce and talk about his trip 47 years earlier. RAA

The *Wrangell Sentinel*
September 5

General Menoker and Captain Ocker flew out to meet the incoming planes at Bolling Field. RAA

Captain Streett and General Pershing in front of Streett's plane at Bolling Field. RAA

Part of the welcoming armada that met the airplanes at Bolling Field. CAM

The reception at Bolling Field, Washington D.C., on Oct. 21, 1920, a few days after completion of the over 9,000-mile round flight to Nome, Alaska, from Long Island, New York. RAA

The Black Wolf Squadron upon its arrival at Bolling Field. From left: Capt. Howard T. Douglas; Lt. C.C. Nutt; Lt. Eric Nelson; Lt. C.E. Crumrine; Lt. Ross C. Kirkpatrick; Sgt. James D. Long and Sgt. Joseph English. Capt. Streett is not shown. UAA, #90-164-06N, BLACK WOLF SQUADRON COLL.

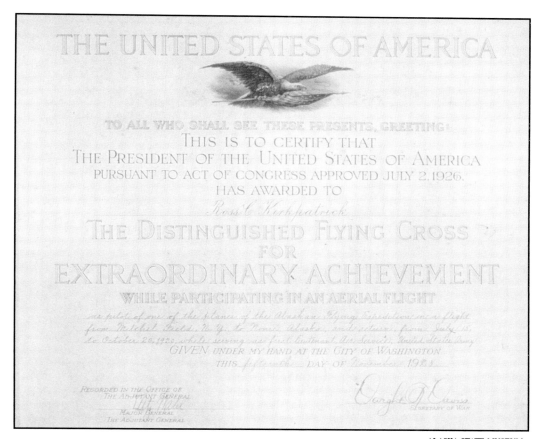

THE UNITED STATES OF AMERICA

TO ALL WHO SHALL SEE THESE PRESENTS, GREETING:

THIS IS TO CERTIFY THAT
THE PRESIDENT OF THE UNITED STATES OF AMERICA
PURSUANT TO ACT OF CONGRESS APPROVED JULY 2, 1926,
HAS AWARDED TO

Ross C. Kirkpatrick

THE DISTINGUISHED FLYING CROSS
FOR
EXTRAORDINARY ACHIEVEMENT
WHILE PARTICIPATING IN AN AERIAL FLIGHT

as pilot of one of the planes of the Alaskan Flying Expedition in a flight from Mitchel Field, N.Y. to Nome, Alaska and return, from July 15 to October 28, 1920, while serving as First Lieutenant, Air Service, United States Army.
GIVEN UNDER MY HAND AT THE CITY OF WASHINGTON
THIS *fifteenth* DAY OF *November* 1921

RECORDED IN THE OFFICE OF
THE ADJUTANT GENERAL

MAJOR GENERAL
THE ADJUTANT GENERAL

SECRETARY OF WAR

Gen. Charles Menoker, commander of the famous Rainbow Division during WWI and chief of the U.S. Army Air Service in 1920, greets Lieutenant Kirkpatrick with Captain Streett behind him. General Pershing is behind Menoker. RAA

ARMY FLIERS HOME FROM ALASKA TRIP

Four Planes Welcomed to Mitchel Field After Successful 9,000-Mile Trip.

BRING BACK DATA FOR MAPS

Motors Never Failed, and Actual Flying Time to Nome Was Only 56 Hours.

Escorted from the city limits by a fleet of thirty-five airplanes, the four United States Army Air Service planes which made a pathfinding flight to Alaska, returned home yesterday afternoon to Mitchel Field, near Garden City, where representatives of the War Department and several hundred spectators gave Captain St. Clair Street, leader of the expedition, and his fellow-aviators a rousing reception. Flying in perfect formation, with the escorting planes high above them, the trail blazers made an interesting sight as they encircled the field before landing.

The flight to Alaska, which ranks among the leading aeronautical exploits of the year, was made in sixteen days, although the actual flying time was fifty-six hours. It required fifteen days to fly back to Mineola.

Expressing enthusiasm over the accomplishments of the aerial survey, Captain Street declared he would recommend to the War Department that the airway to the Northwest be made permanent. With his companions he will leave this morning to fly to Washington, where an official reception has been arranged at Bolling Field.

The planes were laden with gifts and souvenirs the fliers had received at points along the route. They brought back six Eskimo dogs, whose antics, when released from the cockpits of the machines provided the crowd with much amusement.

Captain Street said the planes flew over 300 miles of glaciers and over 2,000 miles of territory which would have required a foot journey of hundreds of miles to the nearest settlement for supplies if a forced landing had been made.

"We maintained an average flying height of 6,000 feet, but sometimes we were compelled to ascend to as high as 12,000 feet and descend to as low as 200 feet," he said. "I believe the airway could be made permanent and successful by establishing a relay system; that is, one plane to fly from one station to another. Our air forces could be mobilized and sent to Alaska in the same time that we took, with an added two-day trip with supplies from Seattle to Cordova, Alaska.

"One thing we discovered when we reached Western Canada, British Columbia, and Alaska, was that the maps were very inaccurate. This is not surprising, as much of the data was furnished by trappers. According to the maps the highest we would have to fly to scale the peaks was 5,100 feet, but there were instances where we had to mount to 12,000 feet to get over. We have very valuable map data which we will furnish to the proper authorities in due time."

When asked what impressed him the most on the trip, the Captain replied with a smile:

"The fact that nearly every one in Alaska runs his own private still. But, seriously, I was most impressed by the interest the people, particularly in Alaska, took in the development of commercial aviation. The people in the Alaskan settlements want aerial service, and a movement is under foot to inaugurate such service. When you consider that it costs from $55 to $65 a ton to transport freight from Seattle to Alaska, plus the charge for carrying it inland, you can see the possibilities of the airplane in reducing this expense.

"We were very lucky in not having forced landings, but this I believe was due to the fact that we were careful to ascertain that everything about the planes were in perfect order before we got away each time. The Liberty engines on the Gallaudet planes we used never missed a cylinder during the entire 9,000-mile trip—a truly marvelous performance when one considers the strain they underwent. We were able to average 80 miles an hour as a result. Incidentally, gasoline in Alaska when we were there was selling at from 90 cents to $1.30 a gallon."

The personnel of the expedition included Captain Street, commanding officer; Captain Howard Douglas, advance officer; First Lieutenants Clifford C. Nutt, Eric H. Nelson, C. H. Crumrine, Ross Kirkpatrick; Sergeants James Long and Joseph E. English.

Sergeant Edmond Henriques, a specialist in Liberty motors who accompanied the party on the initial trip, returned home by train to make a place for Captain Douglas, who had been ordered home.

New York Times
October 21

Fliers Reach New York

MINEOLA, N. Y., Oct. 20—Touching ground at the Mineola Aviation Field at 1:30 o'clock this afternoon, the four United States Army airplanes, comprising the Alaskan Flying Squadron, today completed their record-breaking 9,000 mile flight from New York to Nome, Alaska, and return. The last leg of the long trip was from Erie, N. Y.

Their homecoming was something in the annals of aviation. A great fleet of aircraft—forty or more planes and several dirigibles—flew out to meet the daring pathfinders as they sailed along over the Hudson and escorted them to their landing, while guns boomed and millions of people craned their necks for the first glimpse of the great aerial armada.

Officials of the War Department, Aero Club of America and other military and civil organizations met the expedition at the landing field and showered Capt. St. Clair Streett, commander of the squadron, and his pilots with congratulations. —

Ship Now on Display in Museum at Wright Field.

After gathering dust for years in a remote building of the Smithsonian institute, in Washington, D. C., the DeHaviland airplane in which Capt. St. Clair Streett led the first flight to Alaska back in 1920 has been brought to Dayton and placed on exhibition in the air corps museum at Wright field.

With flat tires, patched fabric and peeling paint, the battered old ship, powered with the famous Liberty motor, is now occupying an honored place in the museum, which will be open to visitors when exhibits are completed.

Stationed Here.

It is fitting that the airplane should be brought here, since three of five officers making the flight—the first to Alaska—have been stationed in Dayton, and because the museum at Wright field is the proper home for all historical exhibits of the air corps.

On the side of the old ship, back near the rudder, is the head of a wolf, facing the tail. That was, in addition to being the insignia of the flight, a symbol of the leader, since the other three craft had wolf heads on their fuselages, but facing forward as if following Captain Streett's airplane.

Captain Streett, who was chief of the flying branch at Wright field, and stationed there from March, 1928, to July, 1932, was accompanied on the epochal flight to the frozen north by Lieutenants C. C. Nutt, R. C. Kirkpatrick, E. H. Nelson and C. E. Crumrine.

At McCook Field.

Lieutenant Nelson, who is now out of the army and associated with an airplane manufacturing concern, was stationed at McCook field from November, 1920, until March, 1925. During his tour of duty here, he also was a member of the army air corps around-the-world flight in 1924. Lieutenant Crumrine was also a resident of Dayton, being a member of the field service section at Wright field from August, 1928, to October, 1932.

Airplanes were an unknown quantity in Alaska when these five officers took off from Mitchel field, N. Y., July 15, 1920. In the north there were no landing fields, no supplies, no facilities which could aid the intrepid pilots.

They were forced to land upon meadows, sand flats, fields of oats —anywhere an airplane could be "set down" without damage beyond repair.

While landing blind at one point, Captain Streett damaged a stabilizer and crushed the left wing of his ship. He pressed a cabinet maker and a tailor into service, to repair the broken struts and set new fabric on the wing. Gun cotton and banana oil were substituted for conventional "dope" to shrink and coat the wing fabric.

Tire Burst.

A tire on another of the airplanes burst on the take-off, and the flyers removed the casing, wrapped rope around the wheel, put the casing back on, and flew on with their makeshift landing gear.

The entire flight was a constant fight against almost unsurmountable odds, but on October 20, 1920, the original group returned to their home station at Mitchel field, after three months, of which 122 hours were actually spent in the air. They visited more than 25 towns and cities in Canada and Alaska, and paved the way for air service to the United States' rich northern territory.

It was through the efforts of Stanley Somers, curator of the museum, that the historical old airplane was secured from the Smithsonian institute, and brought to Dayton, where it will remain permanently.

This newspaper article appeared in the Dayton newspaper in 1935. Unfortunately the plane was placed outside during World War II and was destroyed sometime later.

Recommendation For
Distinguished Flying Cross
for
Captain St. Clair Streett, A.C.

It is herewith recommended that St. Clair Streett, Captain, Air Corps, U.S. Army, present station, Wright Field, Dayton, Ohio, be awarded the Distinguished Flying Cross according to the provisions of Section 12 of the Act of Congress approved July 2, 1926, relating thereto.

The feat performed by Captain Streett meriting this distinction is a flight from Mitchel Field, New York, to Nome, Alaska, and return, accomplished July 15-October 20, 1920. Captain Streett (then Lieutenant) served at this time as flight commander and pilot of Plane No. 1 of the Alaskan Flying Expedition, organized by the Chief of Air Corps, authorized by the War Department and carried out under the direct command of Captain Streett.

Four airplanes manned by four pilots, one assistant-pilot, and three mechanics composed the flight. The pilots were, besides Captain Streett, Lieutenant Clarence E. Crumrine, Lieutenant Clifford C. Nutt, and Lieutenant Ross C. Kirkpatrick. Assistant-pilot, Lieutenant Erik Nelson, also served as engineering officer. The mechanics were Sergeant Edmund Henriques, Sergeant James D. Long, and Sergeant Joseph E. English. This was the first penetration of northern Canada and Alaska by airplane.

With the knowledge that the shortest distance from Asia to the American continent was across Behring Straits, a mere fifty miles of waterway, it was desired to learn the possibilities of aerial travel over this great unmapped region of Alaska and to open up an aerial route to this northwest corner of United States territory. In this remarkable flight a total distance of 9,000 miles was covered in an actual flying time of 112 hours and an elapsed time of ninety-seven days. The average speed during the flight was eighty miles per hour, altitude 6,000 feet, highest altitude 12,500 feet. Liberty engines were used in DH airplanes.

At the time the trip was planned it was a tremendous undertaking. The route lay from Mitchel Field, New York, via Erie, Pa., Grand Rapids, Mich., Winona, Minn., Fargo, N.D.; Saskatoon, Prince George, Hazelton, Wrangell, Whitehorse and Dawson, Canada; Fairbanks, Ruby and Nome, Alaska. The trip afterward was completed only after overcoming many unforeseen obstacles. It was not the day of emergency landing fields or even many prepared main landing fields. There were no improved modern compasses. Fields had to be used in some instances that were covered with water at high tide. More than 2,000 miles of the flight lay over virgin territory far removed from human habitation and known landmarks, over the dreary impenetrable swamps of the Yukon, over jagged mountain peaks and snow-covered glaciers; more than seven thousand miles lay through storm and the airman's greatest menace—fog. That the same planes, the same motors, the same crew landed at Mitchel Field at the close of the arduous journey, especially considering the stage of the aviation art at that time, argues the most distinguished flying.

At all times during the flight, Captain Streett exhibited expert leadership, and the utmost perseverance, fortitude and courage. He had much to do with carrying this ambitious endeavor of the United States Army through to the brilliant and signal success of the expedition that resulted.

****

Captain Streett at the time of the Alaskan flight held the commission of First Lieutenant, United States Army Air Service. He has continued in the service as pilot, having been promoted to Captain, and has ever been a credit to the Air Corps and the United States Army.

****

This flight was a notable one of its time, was followed through its various stages in the public press, was described in detail by all the aeronautical journals, and the fliers received at its completion special commendation from the Chief of the Air Service.

_____
Certificate

I herewith certify that I have read the facts stated above concerning the Alaskan Flight and Captain Streett's part in same, and that they are to my personal knowledge accurate and true.

A postwar view of Maj. Gen. St. Clair Streett. AFM

W. F. Volandt,
Captain, Air Corps, U.S. Army
(Handled finances of flight)

H. Z. Bogert,
1st Lieutenant, Air Corps, U.S. Army
(Bolling Field, 1920 for return of flight)

"Close Up" Pen Pictures of the Alaskan Flight

This description of the New York to Nome flight was written by Lt. Clifford Nutt, second in command of the expedition. It was written on Oct. 23, 1920, just after the round-trip flight was completed. Note that he has misspelled some geographic names and the name of his commander, Captain Streett.

The Alaskan "birdmen," like their kinsmen of the feathered tribe, seemed to take fright, once the great reception and enthusiastic welcome accorded them at Washington was actually over, and scattered like a covey in flight. But two members of the expedition were caught, almost literally "on the wing," namely, Capt. Howard T. Douglas, A.S., who went ahead of the fliers making preliminary arrangements and "blazing the trail" over which the flight was to proceed, and Lieut. Clifford C. Nutt, one of the officers in plane No. 2 from whom these little "close up" pen pictures of the wonderful air journey were made.

"The day we left Mineola, July 15, 1920, was one of the very worst of the whole flight from the standpoint of visibility" said Lieut. Nutt. "We couldn't see the ground from a height of 1,000 feet, so three of the planes dropped to 500. Captain Street, however, lifted to 8,000 feet to get out of the fog, and so got lost from the squadron which proceeded to Erie, where Captain Street joined us next day. Meanwhile, it had rained, the field was wet and muddy; we couldn't get hold of a roller, so we tried to make use of a truck to put the field in shape. But the mud and water stuck by us, and when Crumrine took off he made a nose dive right into the marsh itself. Luckily, however, no one was hurt and no damage was done. Leaving Erie, we cut directly across the lake for 85 miles bucking a strong head wind. For an hour and a quarter we were out of sight of land, and, owing to the haze, we hadn't even a horizon line to guide us. The mist met the water in indistinguishable gray haze into which we ourselves seemed to melt without anything to guide us. Lieut. Nelson was driving at that time and I watched him from the cockpit tipping first one wing and then the other or going nose down under the impression that he was really driving a straight course.

"Grand Rapids, Mich., gave us a royal reception. The whole town seemed to be enthusiastic over aviation. They have a good airdrome inside the race track. At Winona, Minn., we received a request from the Twin Cities Aero Club to land at St. Paul and Minneapolis. This stop at the Twin Cities was the only one made not on our regular route. The hop to Fargo took us out of the forest and lake region into the flat, grain country. The prairies were so level it seemed as if we might have taxied over them. The landing field at Portal was really across the international line, in Canada, or North Portal which is merely a railroad junction. From Portal to Saskatoon was the only leg of the journey in which we had the wind with us. We made the 310 miles in 3 hours, and at Saskatoon got our first taste of that Canadian hospitality which added so tremendously to the enjoyment of the long journey. Almost one-third of the population, though American born, are now Canadians in spirit.

"About 100 miles from Saskatoon we left the prairie country and got into a region of forests and lakes, with low rolling hills, some of them 6,200 feet high. At Edmonton Capt. Street's machine had a leak in the gas tank, and we were held up there for three days getting that patched up. The people at Edmonton are intensely interested in aviation as a means of developing the country. They talked of getting planes to survey the Peace River country to the north of them, a big stretch of arable land now wholly undeveloped, pack mules being the only means of transportation. The transportation to mines of the regio, also offered another opportunity for aviation to exemplify its usefulness.

"Our first attempt to leave Edmonton was unsuccessful because of low hanging clouds. Taking off at 1,000 feet we had to drop to 300, and when about 100 miles out, Street motioned us to return. The next day, in spite of a stiff wind, we made the jump to Jasper Park. This is the Canadian National Park, one of the largest national reserves, by the way, on the Continent, being 400 miles long by 100 wide, abounding with game and its waters, with fish. Here we found one of the best landing fields on the whole route, though it is located about ten miles from Jasper. It is about 600 yds. by 300 and in good condition. Col. Rogers, the warden of the park, met us and extended courtesies and hospitality. Tents were provided for our accommodation with a Chinese cook in the mess tent. Gas and oil were on the field, and after cleaning up our 'busses' and getting everything in shape for the next day, we felt decidedly as if we needed a bath. We set out expecting to take a dip in the Athabasca River, but were warned that we should find the water too cold; so with a guide, we set out for a little lake about a half mile away, which, we were told was a good bathing place. When we were ready for the dip somebody stuck his foot in the water to try the temperature. Well, all I can say is, if the Athabasca River is colder than that little lake was, then it's a record-breaker for temperature. But it was a choice of two evils. We were ready for a bath: we either had to get in the water and take it, cold as it was, or be literally eaten up by mosquitoes. We chose the water. It is impossible to conceive of the multiplicity and ferocity of the mosquitoes in this region; and, indeed, to the very northernmost limit of our flight. They almost 'block traffic,' they are so numerous, and they certainly block progress, preventing work at some seasons of the year. By building smudges around our tents and sitting up around a bonfire for a part of the night, we managed to get a little rest in spite of the mosquitoes, and by getting an early start next morning made two hops that day.

"Soon after the hop-off at Jasper, Capt. Street's machine caught on fire, caused by the oil tanks being too full and overflowing down the exhaust pipe; but Henriques, who was driving, put the plane into a side slip and was going to land in the river, but as they descended, the change of balance had stopped the flow of oil and the fire extinguished itself. We got into Prince George just ahead of a rain-storm and without Street; but a wire from him explained his mishap. We lighted flares to aid him in finding the landing field. The outline of the field was, however, of course indefinite; so when Street alighted he came in with great speed and overshot, rolling out of the dimensions of the field itself into a cut-over stretch beyond where he struck a stump that took off about 4 feet of the end of his left wing, breaking both main spars and tearing all the ribs out, also the left half of his horizontal stabilizer and the aileron. To get a wing sent to us in the quickest possible space of time would take 8 days from Mather Field, Sacramento, Calif., the nearest point available. So we got busy on the job ourselves, with the help of a big Swede carpenter who was a wonder and who had some wonderful spruce timber. He framed up the wing for us, built ribs and spars for the stabilizer and the aileron. Of course, each one of us had a piece of linen for patching: we pooled our supply and covered the wing, but the dope Lieut. Kirkpatrick, the only chemist we had in the party, was able to concoct from cellulose nitrate, unrefined banana oil, and several quarts of anil acetate, proved not very efficacious, as the linen was about as flabby when it dried as it had been before wetting. But, we took a chance on the new wing anyhow. Still another delay held us at Prince George, however, for almost 10 days in all, and we got our first acquaintance with a real frontier town. We got acquainted with hard-boiled miners of the old type, with lumber jacks—great, tall Scotchmen and little French Canadians—who came in about twice a week just for the fun of spending their money. One old fellow, 'Scotty' by name, was about 7 feet tall and weighed 300 pounds, they said, when he was sober. He looked as if he weighed a good deal more drunk, which was all the time, apparently.

"Our next stop was to be at Hazelton, at the head of navigation the Skina River, and, at one time, the main point of distribution for the region beyond. This was prior to the Klondike rush. The trip up was made by boat when the river was open, and beyond on foot and by pack-train. Hazelton is right in the mountains, and these are covered with high timber. Due to the frost; even when the timber is removed and the land plowed level and cultivated during the summer, when it thaws out again next spring, it is as rolling and rough as the waves of the sea. Knowing of these conditions, we went on by train to inspect the landing field before making the jump in our planes. Finding its dimensions inadequate, Capt. Street arranged to have the grain cut from a field adjoining to make room for us to alight with safety.

"Our next jump was to land us in United States territory again, but to reach Wrangell, we had to jump over the Coast Range mountains, at least, that is what we thought we had to do from our maps, which showed the trend of a river or of a mountain system, and depicted everything else as perfectly smooth, level country. In point of fact, the region has never been explored or surveyed. Fortunately, we had a clear day for our take-off. When we began to ascend for our hop over the mountains, we found that the mountains rose too, and higher than we had. Instead of being 5,000 and 7,000 feet as showed on our map, when we reached a height of 7,000 we found we needed 3,000 more to get over the top, and when we tried to skirt the range, we found it wasn't really a range at all with a valley on the other side, but just close packed mountain peaks filled with snow and ice between. These glaciers looked like level seas of dark green water. At Wrangell, the only landing field available was on a little island in the Stickine River, which, at high tide, wasn't an island at all. We landed in about 6 inches of water which had grown to a foot before we took off. From Wrangell we went by way of Chilkoot Pass and Skagway to Whitehorse. This is the region made so famous in the early days of the gold discovery. Formerly it took about three months to make the trip; in winter, travel was by dog-sleds; in summer, on foot or by pack-train. The once famous mines of this region are now inactive. Their surface veins have been stripped, and high-grade mining in this country is too expensive because of inadequate transportation facilities.

"From Whitehorse to Dawson we flew over the route patrolled by the Canadian Mounted Police. The trail runs in almost an air line that shows up practically all of the way, with the neat little road houses dotted at intervals of 40 to 50 miles apart. The Police, in full regalia—bright red jackets and blue trousers—are snappy looking fellows, well-disciplined and giving wonderful service to the country. They were of tremendous assistance to us wherever we encountered them. We crossed Lake La Barge, so well known to readers of Service's poems which breathe the very soul and spirit of this far northern region. This lake is at once the basin of the White River and the source of the Yukon, unless, indeed, it be one and the same river with different names in different localities.

"Crumrine had blown out a tire at Whitehorse, but, filling his casing with rope packed tightly, he wrapped the outside with rope, taking off with us to Dawson, and landing safely despite the hard jolt from his mended tire. We arrived at Dawson, by chance, on August 17, the gala day of the country, "Discovery Day" it is called, for just 22 years before, the first Alaskan gold was discovered on Bonanza Creek. The people made us welcome to their festivities—gave us the town, in fact.

"The principal meat supply of this region is its wild game, chiefly the moose and the caribou. We were there at the season of the caribou 'runs' as they are called. It seems that, as autumn approaches, the caribou begin their annual migration or run. The herds bunch together under a leader, apparently, and, to the number of 200,000 to 300,000 begin their run that stops at nothing, that never turns aside, and that leads nobody knows where. The method of hunting is quite simple. The huntsman selects a spot as near to the trail as he dares to get, takes his stand, and picks off his game as it passes on the run. As it is purely pot-hunting—the game being killed for food—the biggest and fattest bucks are usually the ones killed by the gunner. Nature has provided ample cold storage, so the meat is easily kept.

"The flight to Fairbanks, the northernmost point reached, was over the most desolate region of the entire course. For miles there was no sign of a trail, not even an Indian trail. Then, suddenly we picked up a trail that appeared here and there along the route, quite clear and well-defined. We afterwards learned that General William Mitchell of the Air Service, had led an expedition into this country and cut this trail 20 years ago in making a survey for the purpose of establishing a telegraph line to connect with a cable to Siberia, which project was later abandoned.

"Fairbanks, with a population of 2,000, is the largest town west of Alberta, and the whole town, reinforced by the mining camps of the vicinity, was out to meet us. The route to Ruby was over low hills and swamps. There are no maps of the country, because there has been no survey. It has been impossible to make one. In winter the country is covered with snow and ice, and the only means of travel is on skis. In summer it is covered with tundra and travel is impossible.

"At Ruby we landed on a sand-bar which conveniently appeared in the river at the right time, and proved better for our purposes than the landing field first selected by Capt. Douglas.

"We made the hop to Nome skirting the Bering Sea, with weather conditions changing every hour; keeping in touch by wire with the wireless at Nome, as soon as we got a flash reporting the weather clear, we jumped in our 'boats' and hopped off. We flew at an altitude of 1,000 feet, zigzagging our way to avoid rainstorms. When we saw a fairly clear spot ahead we steered for it, but for the most part it was just steady pushing through black clouds.

"At Golovin Bay, we saw a herd of reindeer, and in Bering Sea we spotted a number of white whales and long-haired seals.

"Our only actual hunting on the trip was to bag a hundred or more ducks, and to kill a black bear. We might have killed caribou, moose, mountain goats and sheep, but there was no reason for it, as we had no means of carrying the game.

"At Fairbanks and Nome we were given many souvenirs, in the way of gold nuggets, and so on. Each of us was presented with a reindeer hide parka, such as the Eskimo wear. Most interesting, however, of the gifts are our Alaskan dogs. My two were given me by Ben Derrick of Ruby, who has carried the mail in that part of the world for years. The dogs are a cross between the gray wolf and the Alaskan husky.

"Capt. Street's dogs were presented to him by Sepalla, one of the Laplanders who came to Alaska with the reindeer which the Government imported from Siberia about 25 years ago, and which have multiplied and become so numerous in Alaska.

"Up to a very few years ago, racing dog teams used to be a famous sport in that region. On the day set the start was made in spite of wind or weather. Sometimes there were as many as 25 dogs to a team and the course would extend 400 miles. It is from this breed of racing huskies that Capt. Street's dogs come.

"Capt. Douglas, to whom is due the credit of making all preliminary arrangements for the flight, confined his remarks to expressions of appreciation for the co-operation and courtesy extended throughout his journey, and that of the expedition, by the Canadian Government, by the Signal Corps and Weather Bureaus of both countries, by municipalities and individual citizens from one end of the route to the other.

"Wherever I went," Capt. Douglas said, "I got acquainted with everybody, I know them—they are my friends, and if I ever go back that way again I'll be mighty glad to shake hands with the men who showed us all so much kindness and hospitality.

"At Dawson the entire party were made honorary members of both the Yukon Pioneers and the Alaskan Pioneers, and at Whitehorse the same distinction was conferred upon us by the 'Squaw Man's Union.'

"The success of the expedition is due in large measure to the hearty co-operation we received everywhere and from everybody."

Streett and Douglas just after landing at Mitchel Field. RAA

Bibliography

Levine, Issac Don, *Mitchell, Pioneer of Air Power,* Duell, Sloan and Pearce, New York, 1943.

Place, Marian T., *New York to Nome, the First International Cross-Country Flight.* Macmillan Co., New York, 1972.

Stevens, Robert W., *Alaskan Aviation History,* Vol. One, 1897-1928, Polynyas Press, Des Moines, Wa., 1990.

Streett, Capt. St. Clair, "The First Alaskan Air Expedition*," National Geographic,* Washington, DC, May 1922.

Newspapers of places along the route were also used.

About the Authors

Stan Cohen has been writing about Alaska/Yukon history since 1977. He established Pictorial Histories Publishing Company in Missoula, Montana, in 1976. His other titles include: *The Streets Were Paved With Gold: A Pictorial History of the Klondike Gold Rush, 1896-1899*; *Rails Across the Tundra: A Pictorial History of the Alaska Railroad*; *Gold Rush Gateway, Dyea and Skagway, Alaska*; *Queen City of the North: A Pictorial History of Dawson City, Yukon*; *The Trail of '42: A Pictorial History of the Alaska Highway*; *Alcan and Canol: Two Great World War Two Construction Projects*; *The Great Alaska Pipeline*; *Flying Beats Work: A Pictorial History of Reeve Aleutian Airways*; *8.6, The Great Alaska Earthquake, March 27, 1964*; *Highway on the Sea: A Pictorial History of the Alaska Marine Highway*; *The Forgotten War: World War Two in Alaska and Northwestern Canada* (four volumes); and *A Klondike Centennial Scrapbook.* He has also published the following: *Alaska Wilderness Rails*; *Koga's Zero*; *Journey to the Koyukuk*; *Top Cover For America*; *Aleutian Warriors*; *The Opening of Alaska* and *Alaska's Wolfman.* He makes his home in Missoula, Montana.

Trelle Morrow has lived all his life in British Columbia and has spent most of his professional career in Prince George as an architect. He is a collector of Canadian Airmail material and has written numerous articles and essays for philatelic journals. His special interest is the aviation history of Central British Columbia, 1920 to 1945, and also collects material and writes essays on the subject.

For a complete catalog of Pictorial Histories titles, please write:

Pictorial Histories Publishing Company
713 South Third
Missoula, Montana 59801
Phone (406) 549-5488
Fax (406) 728-9280
E-mail phpc@montana.com

About the Artist

James H. Farmer's illustrated works have been appearing on Pictorial Histories' volumes for nearly 20 years. Mr. Farmer is also a widely published aviation and film historian in his own right, with three books and hundreds of articles to his credit. The artist received a BA degree in painting and history from the University of California in Berkeley in 1966 and later an MA Degree in Education. He has taught art and painting, variously at the high school, adult and college levels, for the past 32 years. He lives in Glendora, California.